1

Disclaimer

All information contained in this book is given for informational and educational purposes only. The author is not in any way accountable for any results or outcomes that result from using this material. Constructive attempts have been made to
provide accurate and practical information, but the author is not bound for the accuracy or use/misuse of this information.

The Dead Sea Scrolls Collection

The First Bible of All Time

Henrich D. Evans

Contents

Introduction 7

    CONTENTS: 12

GENESIS 17

EXODUS 27

    The laws 39

LEVITICUS 45

NUMBERS 51

1 KINGS 104

    2 KINGS 106

ISAIAH 107

JEREMIAH 113

EZEKIEL 116

The book of the Minor Prophets 119

    Hosea 119

    JOEL 121

    AMOS 123

    OBADIAH 125

    JONAH 126

    MICAH 128

    NAHUM 129

    Habakkuk 130

    ZEPHANIAH 131

    HAGGAI 133

    ZECHARIAH 135

    MALACHI 136

    THE SONGS OF SONGS 137

Introduction

The discovery of the Dead Sea Scrolls in the mid-twentieth century is one of the most significant archaeological finds in human history. The scrolls date back to the time of Jesus and provide valuable insight into Jewish culture during the Second Temple period. Their discovery also shed light on the development of early Christianity. In this essay, we will explore the history of the Dead Sea Scrolls, their contents, their significance, and their impact on religious studies.

History of the Dead Sea Scrolls

The history of the Dead Sea Scrolls is a fascinating one. The scrolls were first discovered in 1947 by a Bedouin shepherd in the vicinity of the Dead Sea. The shepherd was searching for a lost goat and came across a cave that contained a number of clay jars filled with ancient scrolls. The scrolls were eventually sold to antique dealers and made their way into the hands of scholars.

In 1948, a team of scholars from the École Biblique et Archéologique Française in Jerusalem was sent to investigate the discovery further. They discovered more scrolls in the same area and over the next several years, additional caves were explored and more scrolls were found. In total, over 900 scrolls were found in 11 caves in the vicinity of the Dead Sea.

The scrolls date back to the Second Temple period, which lasted from approximately 530 BCE to 70 CE. They are written in Hebrew, Aramaic, and Greek, and include religious and historical texts, as well as legal documents and letters. Some of the most significant texts include portions of the Hebrew Bible, also known as the Old Testament, as well as other Jewish religious texts.

The discovery of the Dead Sea Scrolls was a major breakthrough in the study of Judaism and the history of the ancient Middle East.

The scrolls shed light on the religious beliefs and practices of the Jewish people during the Second Temple period, as well as on the political and social conditions of the time.

Despite their significance, the discovery of the Dead Sea Scrolls was not without controversy. The scrolls were initially kept secret and were not made available to the public or to scholars outside of a small group of individuals who controlled access to the scrolls. This led to accusations of academic elitism and some scholars were critical of the way the scrolls were being handled.

Today, the Dead Sea Scrolls are housed in the Shrine of the Book, a museum in Jerusalem that is dedicated to their preservation and study. The scrolls have been the subject of extensive research and analysis, and they continue to provide scholars with valuable insights into the history and culture of the ancient Middle East.

Contents and Significance of the Dead Sea Scrolls

The Dead Sea Scrolls consist of roughly 900 documents, including biblical texts, non-biblical texts, prayers, and legal documents. The most famous of these texts is the complete scroll of the book of Isaiah, which provides invaluable insight into the origins of the biblical text.

Other important texts include the Manual of Discipline, which lays out the code of conduct for the Essene community, and the War Scroll, which details the apocalyptic battles between the forces of good and evil.

The Dead Sea Scrolls are considered one of the most significant archaeological discoveries of the 20th century. They have provided scholars with a wealth of information on the history and culture of the ancient Middle East, and they have had a profound impact on our understanding of Jewish religious beliefs and practices, the development of the Hebrew Bible, and the origins of Christianity.

Here are some of the key reasons why the Dead Sea Scrolls are so important:

- They shed light on the development of the Hebrew Bible: The scrolls include some of the oldest known copies of portions of the Hebrew Bible, or the Old Testament. These copies predate the previous oldest known copies by over a thousand years, and they provide scholars with valuable insights into the development of the text over time. For example, the scrolls contain versions of the Book of Isaiah that are nearly identical to the modern version of the text, demonstrating the remarkable consistency of the text over time.

- They provide insight into Jewish religious beliefs and practices: The scrolls include a range of religious texts that shed light on the beliefs and practices of the Jewish people during the Second Temple period. For example, the scrolls contain texts related to the practice of ritual purity, which was an important part of Jewish religious practice at the time. They also include texts related to the apocalyptic beliefs of some Jewish groups, which were focused on the end of the world and the coming of a messiah.

- They illuminate the social and political conditions of the Second Temple period: The scrolls contain a range of historical and legal texts that provide insight into the social and political conditions of the Second Temple period. For example, the scrolls contain references to various Jewish sects and groups, including the Essenes, who are thought to have been the authors of many of the scrolls. They also include documents related to the governance of the Jewish community, such as temple tax records and contracts.

- They provide insight into the origins of Christianity: Some of the texts found among the Dead Sea Scrolls are thought to have influenced the development of early Christianity. For example, some scholars have suggested that the scrolls contain references to John the Baptist and may shed light on the relationship between John and Jesus. Other scholars have suggested that the scrolls contain texts that are similar to some of the teachings of Jesus and may provide insight into the origins of his teachings.

The Dead Sea Scrolls were written in Hebrew, Aramaic, and Greek, and cover a wide range of topics, including religious texts, historical documents, legal agreements, and personal letters. Some of the of documents found among the Dead Sea Scrolls include:

- Biblical texts: The Dead Sea Scrolls include copies of many of the books of the Hebrew Bible, including the Torah, the Prophets, and the Writings. Some of the most significant finds include the Great Isaiah Scroll, which contains the entire book of Isaiah, and the Copper Scroll, which contains a list of hidden treasures.
- Non-Biblical religious texts: The scrolls also contain many non-Biblical religious texts, such as the Manual of Discipline, which provides instructions for the conduct of the members of a religious community, and the War Scroll, which describes a final battle between the forces of good and evil.
- Historical documents: The scrolls include many historical documents, such as the Damascus Document, which outlines the history and beliefs of a Jewish sect known as the Essenes, and the Community Rule, which describes the organization and governance of a religious community.
- Legal agreements: The scrolls include many legal agreements, such as marriage contracts and property deeds.
- Personal letters: The scrolls also contain many personal letters, such as the Letter of Aristeas, which describes the translation of the Hebrew Bible into Greek.

Impact of the Dead Sea Scrolls

The Dead Sea Scrolls also serve as a reminder of the importance of preserving history and cultural heritage. The scrolls were preserved for centuries in the caves of Qumran, and their discovery has opened up a new avenue of research into the ancient world.

The discovery of the Dead Sea Scrolls has had a significant impact on a variety of fields, including archaeology, history, religion, and biblical studies.

First of all, as previously stated, the scrolls have helped to illuminate the social and political conditions of the Second Temple period, including the organization and governance of the Jewish community, the relationship between different Jewish sects, and the role of the region in the broader political and cultural context of the ancient Near East.

This has allowed scholars to gain new insights into the religious beliefs and practices of the Jewish people during the Second Temple period. The scrolls shed light on the diversity of Jewish religious beliefs at the time, and they provide valuable information about the role of ritual purity and other religious practices.

Furthermore, the Dead Sea Scrolls have provided scholars with a wealth of new information about the history and development of the Hebrew Bible as the scrolls include some of the oldest known copies of portions of the Hebrew Bible, which provide important insights into the textual and linguistic history of the biblical texts.

The discovery has also led to new archaeological discoveries in the region. In fact, the scrolls were found in caves near the site of Qumran, which has been the subject of extensive archaeological research in recent years.

CONTENTS:

The Dead Sea Scrolls include several important Biblical texts that were previously unknown or only partially known from earlier manuscripts. Here are some of the most significant Biblical texts found among the Dead Sea Scrolls:

- The Great Isaiah Scroll: This scroll contains a complete copy of the book of Isaiah, which is one of the most important prophetic books in the Hebrew Bible. The text is written in Hebrew, and is believed to date from the second century BCE.
- The Psalms Scrolls: The Dead Sea Scrolls contain several scrolls that contain portions of the book of Psalms. These texts include some of the earliest known copies of these texts, and provide important insights into the development of the Psalms as a literary genre.
- The Temple Scroll: This scroll contains a detailed description of a temple that was believed to be located in Jerusalem, and provides instructions for the construction and operation of the temple. The scroll includes many ritual laws and regulations, and sheds light on the importance of ritual purity in Jewish religious practice.
- The Genesis Apocryphon: This scroll contains an Aramaic retelling of the story of Genesis, and includes several episodes that are not found in the standard version of the Hebrew Bible. The text sheds light on the diversity of Jewish religious beliefs at the time, and provides insights into the ways in which Jewish communities were interpreting and retelling the stories of the Bible.

The Dead Sea Scrolls also include a number of non-Biblical texts that provide valuable insights into the religious beliefs and practices of the Jewish community during the Second Temple period. These texts include religious, literary, and historical works, and provide a window into the diversity of Jewish religious thought and practice; they have shed light on the ways in which Jewish communities were interpreting and reinterpreting traditional religious texts and beliefs during this period.

Here are some of the most significant non-Biblical texts found among the Dead Sea Scrolls:

- The War Scroll: This scroll is a military manual that describes a final apocalyptic battle between the forces of good and evil. The text provides detailed instructions for the preparation and conduct of the battle, and reflects a belief in a coming Messiah who would lead the forces of good to victory.
- The Community Rule: This text describes the religious practices and beliefs of a Jewish sect that is believed to have lived at Qumran, the site where the Dead Sea Scrolls were discovered. The text includes detailed instructions for communal living, religious observance, and the pursuit of spiritual perfection.
- The Rule of the Blessing: This text is a liturgical work that describes the daily prayers and rituals of a Jewish community. The text includes blessings for various occasions, and reflects a belief in the importance of prayer and ritual in the pursuit of spiritual perfection.
- The Hymns and Thanksgiving Psalms: These texts are a collection of religious poems and hymns that express praise and thanksgiving to God. The texts include descriptions of mystical experiences, and reflect a belief in the importance of personal spiritual growth and development.

Furthermore, The Dead Sea Scrolls contain a number of historical documents that shed light on the political and social history of the Jewish community during the Second Temple period. Here are some of the most significant historical documents found among the Dead Sea Scrolls:

- The Copper Scroll: This is a unique document that is inscribed on copper plates and provides a list of buried treasure. The text includes detailed descriptions of the location and contents of the treasure, and reflects a belief in the importance of material wealth as a sign of God's favor.
- The War of the Sons of Light Against the Sons of Darkness: This text describes a final apocalyptic battle between the forces of good and evil, and provides a detailed account of the political and social context in which the battle would take place.

The text reflects a belief in the importance of political and military action in the pursuit of spiritual goals, and provides insight into the ways in which Jewish communities were interpreting and reinterpreting traditional religious texts and beliefs during this period.

- The Rule of the War: This text is a military manual that provides detailed instructions for the preparation and conduct of battle. The text reflects a belief in the importance of military action in the pursuit of spiritual goals, and provides insight into the ways in which Jewish communities were interpreting and reinterpreting traditional religious texts and beliefs during this period.

The historical documents found among the Dead Sea Scrolls provide evidence of the existence of different Jewish sects and communities, and shed light on the ways in which these communities were responding to the political and social challenges of the time. The texts also provide a glimpse into the religious and cultural beliefs of these communities, and the ways in which they were interpreting and reinterpreting traditional Jewish texts and beliefs.

The Dead Sea Scrolls also incorporate a number of legal agreements, which provide insight into the legal and social structures of the Jewish community during the Second Temple period. These documents include:

- The Community Rule: This document outlines the rules and regulations governing the community that produced the Dead Sea Scrolls. It includes detailed instructions for the organization and administration of the community, including rules for admission, daily life, and the distribution of resources. The Community Rule reflects the religious and social ideals of the community, and provides insight into the ways in which these ideals were put into practice.
- The Rule of the Congregation: This document provides rules and regulations for the conduct of worship and ritual within the community. It includes instructions for the observance of the Sabbath, the festivals, and other religious ceremonies, and reflects the community's commitment to the strict observance of Jewish law and custom.

- The Damascus Document: This document outlines the history, beliefs, and practices of a Jewish sect known as the "Sons of Zadok." It includes rules and regulations governing the conduct of the sect, and reflects the community's belief in the importance of strict adherence to Jewish law and custom.

Finally, the Dead Sea Scrolls contain a number of personal letters, which offer a glimpse into the daily lives and concerns of the Jewish community during the Second Temple period. These letters are often fragmentary, and some are difficult to interpret, but they provide valuable insight into the social and economic conditions of the period.

Some of the personal letters found among the Dead Sea Scrolls are written by members of the community to family members or friends, providing information about personal matters such as health, travel plans, and family events. Others are business letters or receipts, providing evidence of economic activities and commercial transactions in the region.

One particularly interesting personal letter is the so-called "Letter of Aristeas," which provides an account of the translation of the Hebrew Bible into Greek, a process known as the Septuagint. The letter is addressed to a Greek king, and describes the process by which 72 Jewish scholars were brought together to translate the Hebrew Bible into Greek. The letter provides valuable information about the historical context and cultural background of the Septuagint, and sheds light on the ways in which the Jewish community was interacting with the broader Hellenistic culture of the time.

Conclusion

In conclusion, the Dead Sea Scrolls are a remarkable archaeological find that provide valuable insight into the religious, social, and political world of the Second Temple period. Their discovery has had a profound impact on religious studies and archaeology, and their significance cannot be overstated. The scrolls continue to provide new information for scholars to study, and will undoubtedly remain an area of intense interest and research for the foreseeable future.

GENESIS

Genesis is a book about beginnings and genealogy, as the name suggests. This is evidenced by the large number of biblical manuscripts and the collection of scrolls used in retelling its compelling stories.

Although a scroll containing all of Moses' books (Genesis through Deuteronomy) would not have been typical—it would have to be nearly five times the length of the Great Isaiah Scroll—at least two scrolls exist that contain both Genesis and Exodus, confirming an ancient order for these two essential books. Furthermore, while Genesis' twenty-four manuscripts are second only to Psalms, Isaiah, and Deuteronomy in terms of number, they are all relatively fragmentary, preserving only thirty-two chapters among their crumbs. However, they reveal a Genesis text that is remarkably similar to the traditional Hebrew version.

In the beginning

God created the heavens and the earth in the beginning. And the earth was formless and void, with darkness on the face of the deep and the Spirit of God moving over the waters. "Let there be light," God said, and there was light. And when God saw that the light was good, he separated it from the darkness. The light was called daytime, and God called the darkness night. And in one day, there was an evening and a morning.

"Let there be a firmament in the midst of the waters, dividing [the waters from the waters," God said. And God [created] the firmament, dividing the waters [below the firmament] from the waters [above the firmament]. That was the case. God gave the firmament the name heaven. There was also an evening and a morning, a second day.

"Let the waters beneath the heavens be gathered into one gathering, and let the dry land appear," God said. That was the case. And the waters beneath the heavens gathered, and the dry land appeared. God gave the dry land the name earth, and the gathering of the waters was given the name seas, and God saw that it was good.

"Let the earth produce grass, herbs yielding seed, and fruit trees bearing fruit after their kind, with seed in them," God said.

That was the situation. And the earth gave birth to grass, herbs that produce seed after their kind, and trees that bear fruit that contains seed after their kind. It was pleasing to God. Then there was the third day, which consisted of [evening] and [morning].

"Let there be lights in the firmament of heaven to separate the day from the night; and they shall be for signs, seasons, days, and years; and they shall be for lights in the firmament of heaven to give light upon the earth," God said. That was the situation. God also made the two great lights, one for the day and the other for the night and the stars. And God put [them] in the firmament of heaven to give light to the earth, to rule over day and night, and to separate] light from darkness, and God saw that it was good. It was also the fourth day because there was an evening and a morning.

God said, "Let the waters teem with life, and let birds fly above the earth in the open firmament of heaven." And God made the great sea monsters, as well as every moving creature that the waters swarmed with, and every [winged] bird according to its nature. It was pleasing to God. God blessed them by saying, "Be fruitful and multiply, [and] fill the seas, and the birds shall multiply on the earth." Then there was the fifth day, which included both evening and morning.

God instructed, "Let the earth bring forth living creatures after their kind, cattle and creeping things, and earth beasts after their kind." And God created the earth's beasts and cattle, as well as anything that creeps on the planet, in their own species. And it was good in God's eyes.

"Let us make humankind in our image, after our likeness, and give them dominion over the sea creatures, the birds of the heavens, the earth, and every creeping thing that creeps upon the earth," God said. And God created male and female humankind in his image, in God's image. "Be fruitful and multiply, replenish the world, and subdue it," [God] said, "and have authority over sea beings, birds of the heavens, and all living things that pass upon the earth."

And the heavens, the earth, and all their hosts were completed. God completed the work he had made on the seventh day and rested from all the work he had made on the seventh day. And God blessed and sanctified the seventh day because he rested from all the work God had created and made on it.

However, a mist used to rise from the ground and water the entire surface. And the Lord God created [man from the dust of the earth, inhaling the breath of life into his nostrils, and man became a living being. The third [river] is known as the Tigris and flows east of Assyria. The Euphrates is the fourth river. And the Lord God took the man and placed him in the Garden of Eden to maintain and cultivate it. "Of every tree in the garden, you may freely eat; but of the tree of the knowledge of good and evil, you shall not eat from it, for [in the day] that you eat from it, you shall surely die," the Lord God commanded the man. "It is not good [for the man to be alone;] I will make him a partner for him," the Lord God said. And the Lord God formed [every beast of the field and every bird of the] sky out of the ground and brought them to man to see what he would call them, and whatever the man called a living creature was its name.

The serpent was now more cunning than any beast of the field created by the Lord God. And he asked her, "Has God said, 'You shall not eat of any tree in the garden?'" "We may eat from the fruit of the garden trees," the woman told the serpent.

"Who told you that you were naked?" he asked. Have you eaten from the tree that I forbade you from eating?" "The woman whom you gave to be with me, she gave me of the tree, and I ate," the man said. "What have you done?" the Lord God inquired of the woman. ["The serpent deceived me, and I ate,"] the woman said. "Because you have done this, cursed are you more than all cattle, and more than every beast of the field; upon your belly shall you go, and dust shall you eat all [the] days of your life," the Lord God said to the serpent.

The woman gave birth to a child named Cain.

She gave birth to his brother Abel once more. Cain was a tiller of the ground, while Abel was a flock keeper. And Cain brought an offering to the Lord from the fruit of the ground over time. Abel also brought his flock's firstlings as well as their fat portions. And the Lord looked favorably on Abel and his offering, but he did not look favorably on Cain and his offering. Cain was enraged and had a gloomy expression on his face. "Why are you angry, and why is your face downcast?" the Lord asked Cain. "Will you be rejected if you perform well? And if you don't do well, sin will come knocking: its desire is to have you, but you must rein it in."

Cain then told Abel about his brother. And while they were out in the field, Cain rose up against his brother Abel and killed him. "Where is your brother Abel?" the Lord asked Cain. And he replied, "I'm not sure; am I my brother's keeper?" "What have you done?" he asked. From the ground, your brother's blood is crying out to me. "From the ground, which has opened its mouth to receive your brother's blood from your hand, you are now cursed."

Kenan lived for another eight hundred and forty years after Mahalalel was born and had other sons and daughters. Kenan lived for nine hundred and ten years, and then he died. And Noah built an altar to the Lord and offered burnt offerings on the altar from every clean beast and every clean bird. And the Lord inhaled the pleasant aroma, and in his heart, he said, "I will never again curse the ground because of man, for man's heart is evil from his youth; nor will I again destroy every living thing, as I have done."

Chapter 5-6

And every male throughout your generations shall be circumcised, whether born in the house or bought with money from a foreigner who is not of your offspring. Anyone born in your home or purchased with your money must be circumcised. My covenant will be in your flesh for an everlasting covenant. And any uncircumcised male who has not had his foreskin flesh circumcised will be cut off from his people. He's broken my agreement. "As for Sarai, your wife," God said to Abraham, "you shall not call her Sarai, but Sarah." And I'll bless her and give you one of her sons. She will be a mother to many nations, and I will bless her. She will produce kings for the people."

"Shall a hundred-year-old child be born to him?" Abraham asked in his heart as he fell on his face and laughed. Is it possible for Sarah to have a child at the age of ninety?" "How I wish Ishmael had lived before you!" God, Abraham exclaimed. "No," God replied, "but Sarah, your wife, will bear you a son, whom you shall name Isaac." And I'll make my agreement with him an everlasting agreement for his descendants."

"Because the cry of Sodom and Gomorrah is great, and their sin is very grievous, I will go down now and see whether they have done as badly as its outcry, which has come to me," the Lord said. And if not, I'll let you know. The men then turned around and headed for Sodom. But Abraham continued to stand before the Lord. "Will you destroy the righteous with the wicked?" Abraham asked as he approached. "Assume that the city has fifty righteous people. Will you destroy the place and not spare the fifty righteous people who live there? Far be it from you to do this, slay the righteous alongside the wicked, and treat the righteous as the wicked. It's not going to happen. Isn't it right for the Whole World Judge to do the right thing?"

And Abraham got up early the following day and went to where he had stood before the Lord. And he saw, and behold, the smoke of the land went up like the smoke of a furnace as he looked toward Sodom and Gomorrah and all the land of the Plain. Abraham raised his eyes and looked behind him, and there was a ram caught in the thicket by his horns. And Abraham took the ram and sacrificed him instead of his son as a burnt offering.

These are Esau's generations now (that is, Edom). Adah, the daughter of Elon the Hittite, Oholibamah, the daughter of Anah and granddaughter of Zibeon the Hivite, and Basemath, Ishmael's daughter, sister of Nebaioth, were among Esau's wives. And Adah gave birth to Esau's son Eliphaz; Basemath gave birth to Reuel; Oholibamah gave birth to Jeush, Jalam, and Korah: these are Esau's sons who were born in the land of Canaan.

And Esau took his wives, sons, daughters, and all the members of his household, along with his cattle, all his beasts, and all his possessions that he had gathered in the land of Canaan, and fled from his brother Jacob to a land far away.

Because their possessions were too numerous for them to live together, and the land they were living in could not support them due to their livestock, they were forced to flee. And Esau lived in Seir's hill country; Esau's name is Edom.

Chapter 7

And Jacob lived in Canaan, the land of his father's sojourn. These are Jacob's generations. Joseph, seventeen years old at the time, was feeding the flock with his brothers; he grew up with Bilhah's sons and Zilpah's sons, sons of his father's wives. And Joseph brought their father a bad report about them. And Joseph had a dream, which made his brothers hate him even more, when he told them about it. "Please listen to this dream that I had," he said to them. And Reuben said to them, "Shed no blood; throw him into this wilderness pit, but lay no hand on him," so that he could save him and return him to his father. When Joseph arrived at his brothers' house, they stripped him of his coat—the coat of many colors that he wore—and threw him into the pit. There was no water in the pit, and it was empty.

After that, they sat down to eat their meal. And they raised their eyes and looked, and behold, a caravan of Ishmaelites from Gilead was approaching, with their camels bearing spices, balm, and myrrh, on their way to Egypt. "What good will it do us to kill our brother and hide his blood?" Judah questioned his brothers. Let us sell him to the Ishmaelites without touching him; he is our flesh and blood." And his brothers listened to everything he had to say. When Midianite merchants passed by, they dragged Joseph from the pit and sold him for twenty pieces of silver to the Ishmaelites. They took Joseph to Egypt after that.

When Reuben returned to the pit, he discovered Joseph's clothes had been torn, and he was no longer in it. He explained to his brothers, "The boy isn't there, and I, where shall I go?" Around this time in Egypt, Joseph went to the house to do his work, but none of the men of the house were present. "Lie with me," the woman said as she grabbed his garment. And he dashed away, leaving his garment in her grip. "See, he has brought in a Hebrew to take advantage of us," she told her household's men when she noticed he had left his garment in her hand and fled. When he came in to lie with me, I screamed. He left his garment by my side and ran away when he heard me scream and call out." And until his master returned home, she wore his garment.

Chapter 8

Following these events, the king of Egypt's cupbearer and baker offended their lord, the king of Egypt. "This is its interpretation: the three branches are three days; Pharaoh shall lift up your head and restore you to your office within three more days; and you shall give Pharaoh's cup into his hand, as you did when you were his cupbearer," Joseph said.

"Its interpretation is that the three baskets represent three days," Joseph responded. Pharaoh will remove your head from your shoulders and hang you from a tree for three days, where the birds will eat your flesh. On the third day, Pharaoh's birthday, he threw a feast for all his servants, and among his servants, he lifted up the heads of the chief cupbearer and chief baker. And he returned the chief cupbearer to his cup-bearing duties, handing the cup to Pharaoh; but, as Joseph had predicted, he hanged the chief baker. Despite this, Joseph had been forgotten by the chief cupbearer.

In his dream, Pharaoh was standing by the river at the end of two years. Seven sleek and fat cows emerged from the reeds, and I was astounded. Seven more cows, ugly and thin, emerged from the river and stood alongside the other cows on the riverbank. And the ugly and gaunt cows devoured the seven sleek and fat cows. Pharaoh awoke as a result. And he slept and dreamed some more, and lo, seven healthy ears of grain appeared on one stalk. The east wind blew seven ears up the mountain behind them. And the ears, which were thin and blasted by the east wind, swallowed the seven healthy and full ears. It was all a dream when Pharaoh awoke. And the following day, when his spirit was troubled, he sent and summoned all of Egypt's magicians and wise men. Pharaoh also told them about his dreams, but no one was able to interpret them. "I remember my sins this day: ten," the chief cupbearer addressed Pharaoh. Pharaoh was enraged by his servants, and he imprisoned me and the chief baker in the captain of the guard's house. And we both had a dream on the same night, I and he; we each dreamed according to the interpretation of his dream. Pharaoh told Joseph, "I have had a dream that no one can interpret," and "I have been told of you that when you hear a dream, you can interpret it."

Chapter 9

Joseph told Pharaoh, "The dreams of Pharaoh are the same; what God is about to do, he has declared to Pharaoh." The dreams of the seven good cows and the seven good ears are the same: they are both seven years. The seven lean and ugly cows that followed them and the seven empty ears blown by the east wind will last seven years; they will be seven years of famine. That's what I told Pharaoh because God has already shown him what he's about to do. Seven years of great abundance are coming to all of Egypt, followed by seven years of famine, and all of Egypt's abundance will be forgotten, and the famine will destroy [the land]. And the land will forget about the abundance because of the severe famine that will follow. God has decreed it and will soon bring it to pass, which is why the dream was repeated to Pharaoh. As a result, Pharaoh should seek out and appoint a wise and discerning man to rule Egypt.

The plan was thought to be suitable by Pharaoh and all of his servants. "Can we find someone like this, a man imbued with the gods' spirit?" Pharaoh had inquired of his servants. Pharaoh told Joseph, "Since God has shown you all of this, there is no one more discerning and wise than you." "You will be the ruler of my household, and all of my people will follow your orders. Only when I am on the throne will I be greater than you." Pharaoh told Joseph, "See, I have given you command over all of Egypt." Pharaoh then placed his signet ring on Joseph's finger and dressed him in fine linen robes with a gold necklace around his neck. And he made him ride in his second chariot while they cried out in front of him, "Bow the knee!" He also gave him the authority to rule over all of Egypt. "I am Pharaoh, and no one shall lift up his hand or foot in all of Egypt without you," Pharaoh told Joseph.

And there was a severe famine in the country. "Go back and buy us a little more food," their father said after consuming all of the grain they had brought out of Egypt. We will not go down if you do not send him because the man told us, "You shall not see my face unless your brother is with you." "Why did you mistreat me by telling the man you had another brother?" Israel asked. "The man asked specifically about our family and us, saying, 'Is your father still alive?'" they said. 'Do you have a second brother?' And we responded to his inquiries.

How could we have predicted him saying, 'Bring your brother down?' "Send the boy with me, and we will arise and go; that we may live and not die, we and you, and our little ones," Judah said to Israel, his father. You may hold me responsible because I will be surety for him. Let me bear the blame for the rest of my life if I don't return him to you and put him in front of you. We could have returned twice by now if we hadn't waited so long."

"If it must be so, take some of the best fruits of the land in your vessels and take them down to the man as a present, a little balm, a little honey, spices and myrrh, nuts, and almonds," their father Israel instructed them. And take twice as much money in your hand, plus the money that was returned in the mouths of your sacks. It could have been a mistake. And take your brother, arise, and return to the man; and may God Almighty grant you mercy before the man, that he may release your other brother and Benjamin to you.

And thus did the Israelites, and Joseph provided them bread and grain as commanded. He provided Benjamin with three hundred and five hundred silver pieces for each of his clothing. Also, he sent his father ten donkeys loaded with Egyptian treasures, grain and ten females carrying the provisions. They said, "Joseph is still alive and rules over all of Egypt." He didn't believe their lies. And so they recounted everything Joseph had told them, and their father's son, Jacob, returned from the dead. Israel answered, "Joseph, my son, you will see me before I die.

Joseph lived to be a hundred years old and died in Egypt.

EXODUS

Exodus, the Bible's second book, tells of God's rescue of Israel from Egypt, the giving of the Law, and the construction of the Tabernacle. This account of Israel's history, with its central figure, Moses the Lawgiver, is as compelling today as it was two thousand years ago. What do the Dead Sea Scrolls say about this crucial ancient document?

The eighteen Exodus manuscripts attest to this book's popularity in the Qumran community, outnumbering only Genesis, Deuteronomy, Isaiah, Psalms, and 1 Enoch among the biblical manuscripts.

Exodus, like the manuscripts of Genesis, adds to the evidence that the Torah's five books were frequently copied together in the same scroll. Two scrolls preserve portions of Genesis, and one demonstrates that Leviticus followed Exodus. The remains of the scroll from Wadi Murabba'at include Genesis and Numbers fragments in addition to Exodus.

Chapter 1-2

These are the names of Israel's sons who accompanied their father, Jacob, to Egypt, each with his household. Simeon, Levi, Judah, Issachar, Zebulun, Benjamin, Dan and Naphtali, Gad, and Asher.

And there were seventy-five souls in all who came from Jacob's loins. And [Joseph] died, as did all of his brethren and the entire generation. And the children of Israel multiplied and multiplied, and they became exceedingly mighty, and the land overflowed with them.

Now a new king of Egypt arose who had never heard of Joseph. "Behold, the people of the children of Israel are more and mightier than us," he told his people. "Come, let us deal wisely with them; otherwise, they will multiply, and when a war breaks out, they will join our enemies, fight against us, and flee the land." As a result, they appointed taskmasters to afflict them with their burdens. Pithom and Raamses were built as store cities for Pharaoh. However, the more they afflicted them, the more they multiplied and grew significantly. And they were terrified [because of Israel's children].

And the Egyptians made [the children of] Israel [serve with] rigor; and he made their lives bitter with hard service, in mortar and brick, and all manner of field service, all of which they forced them to serve with rigor.

And there went a man from Levi's house, who took Levi's daughter as his wife. And the woman conceived and gave birth to a son, and when she saw that he [was a lovely child], she hid him for three months. When she could no longer hide him, she to [took an ark of bulrushes for him,] daubed it with slime and pitch, put the child in it, and said to her servant, "Go," and she hid it in the reeds near the river's edge. And his sister stood at a distance, waiting to see what would happen to him.

And the daughter of the Pharaoh went down to bathe herself and sent her handmaid to get it. And when she opened it, she saw the child was crying. And the daughter of Pharaoh could tell that he was Hebrew. His sister asked him, "Do you want me to call you a nurse from the Hebrew women? A mysterious woman said, "Go; the child's mother subsequently returned. Pharaoh's daughter said, "Feed this child for me, and I'll pay you." And the woman nourished it. And he grew up and was given to the princess who married him. Because he drew him out of the water, she called him Moses.

After those many days, Moses went out to his brethren to examine their burdens, and he saw an Egyptian striking a Hebrew, one of his brethren. And he looked around, and when he couldn't find anyone, he struck the Egyptian and hid him in the sand. And on the second day, he went out, and behold, two Hebrew were fighting, and he said to the one who had done the wrong, "Why do you strike your fellow?" "Who made you a prince and a judge over us?" he asked. "Are you planning to assassinate me like you did the Egyptian?" And Moses, terrified, exclaimed, "Surely the thing is known." When Pharaoh learned of this, he set out to kill Moses. But Moses ran away from Pharaoh and went to Midian, where he sat down by a well.

Chapter 3

Now it was Moses' wife's father-in-in-law, the Midianite priest, who was looking after the sheep of Midian. And out of the midst of a fire appeared the Lord's messenger. But when he did, the bush didn't catch fire. "Now, I shall pass over and see this amazing sight." And when the LORD saw that He turned to look, He called out to him, "Moses, Moses" He said, "I am."

"I give a land flowing with honey and plentiful [and good land that flows with milk and honey for the descendants of the Israelite. And now, my people's cry has reached me, and I have witnessed the Egyptians' cruelty. So, get thee out, and I will send you to Pharaoh so he may let my people go." "Who am I to go to Pharaoh and bring the children of Israel out of him?" God said, "No. Of course, I will be with you, and this shall be your gift: You must bring the Israelites out of Egypt and serve God on this mountain."

"Behold, when I go to the children of Israel and tell them, 'The God of your fathers has sent me to you,' they will say to me, 'What is his name?' What am I going to say to them?" "I AM THAT I AM," God said to Moses. "Thus, you shall say to the children of Israel, 'I AM THAT I AM sent me to you,'" he continued. "That you shall say to the children of Israel, 'The Lord, the God of your fathers, the God of Abraham, Isaac, and Jacob, has sent me to you; this is my name forever, and this is my memorial to all generations,'" God also said to Moses. 'The Canaanite King, whom you were enslaving saw has once and said to you, "Come, present your petitions before me," but you must speak face to face to the pharaohs and the elders of Israel and say, "The Lord, the God of our forefathers, the God of Abraham and Isaac and Jacob, I want to make a journey to go and sacrifice in the wilderness for Him,"' To sum up, I believe the Egyptian king will force you to stay. And I will unleash all of my miraculous wonders on you, and then he will release you. As a result, the Egyptians will see me as well-liked as I see you.

Moses replied, "However, Behold, they will not believe nor listen to me because the Lord has not revealed himself to you. "Is that a staff?" Indeed." Let it go, he said. And the staff transformed into a snake, and Moses fled.

The Lord said to Moses, "let all the people put their hands together and hold on the rod that He may believe that the God of their fathers, the God of Abraham, Isaac, and Jacob, has appeared to you."

Moses told Aaron all of the Lord's terms and instructions. The elders and the people rose to meet Moses and Aaron, and everyone had gathered around the Lord in the wilderness, and when they found out that the Lord had come among them, they prostrated themselves in worship.

Chapter 4

Next, they informed Pharaoh, "Let me go so that my people may send a gift to my parents." They weren't allowed to leave. The taskmasters told the people to collect some of the straw for themselves. When the people made brick, the pharaoh told them to discontinue. The taskmasters were ordered to go out and acquire straw, but the officers were only told to do the same.

When they met, Moses was eighty, and Aaron was eighty-three. As commanded by God, Moses and Aaron went in front of Pharaoh. Aaron's rod turned into a snake, but Moses' did not. He hardened Pharaoh's heart, and he did not listen to them. God said, "Pharaoh's heart was unyielding" Go to Pharaoh in the morning; you will find him standing by the banks of the Nile.'" Hold a rod in your hand and tell him, The Lord of the Hebrews has sent me, that his people may serve him in the wilderness. Finally, you've acknowledged it. God declares this shall indicate that I am the Lord: I will strike the water in the Nile with a rod. "It will turn red (blood)."

So God spoke to Moses, "Go to Pharaoh, and tell him to let my people go so that they can serve me." If you do not let them go, I will plague your country with frogs, and the Nile will swarm with frogs, which will go into your home, bedroom, and bed, into your servants' home, and into your ovens, and your grain. The Lord said to Moses, "Say to Aaron, 'Stretch out your hand with your rod [over the rivers, over the streams, and the pools, and make] frogs come up on the land of Egypt.'" Moses told Aaron to stretch out his hand and bring up frogs from the Nile. And Aaron stretched out his hand over the waters of Egypt. And Moses said to Pharaoh, "As you want, but just be sure the frogs are not gone because they will be turning against you and your houses." He said, "Tomorrow." And the Lord said, "There is none like you; you are a God of wonders, a God of miracles. The frogs shall leave your country, house, servants, and people. They shall only be in the Nile." And Moses and Aaron went out from Pharaoh. Moses cried to the Lord about the frogs. "The frogs died out of the houses, out of the courts, and out of the fields."

And they gathered them together, heaps of them. But when Pharaoh saw that there was relief, [he hardened his heart and did not listen to them, as] the Lord had spoken.

"Say to Aaron, 'Stretch out your hand with your rod, and strike the dust of the earth.' And it shall become lice throughout all the land of Egypt." And they did so, and Aaron stretched out his rod and struck the dust of the earth, and all the lice in the land of Egypt became lice throughout all the land of Egypt. And the magicians tried to bring forth lice, but they could not, and there were lice upon man and beast. "This is the hand of God," the magician said to Pharaoh. But Pharaoh's heart was hardened, and he did not listen to them. Then the Lord spoke to Moses, saying, "Get up early in the morning and stand before Pharaoh and say to him, 'Thus says the Lord: Let My people go, that they may serve Me.' The Lord will send swarms of flies against you and your servants and your people into your houses, the houses of the Egyptians, and the ground where they are will be full of flies. As for my people, I will make a paradise of the land of Goshen, where my people dwell so that no flies shall settle there. I am in the land. And I will distinguish my people from your people. 'This will happen tomorrow.'

The Lord said to Moses and Aaron, "Please let my people go so they can serve me, for if you do not let my people go and you still hold on to them, the hand of the Lord will be severe on your livestock in the field, on the horses and the donkeys and the camels; grave is the matter. And the Lord will make a distinction between the livestock of Israel and the livestock of Egypt. Nothing will be spared. The Lord will do this thing in the land." And all the cattle of the Egyptians died, but not one of the cattle of the children of Israel died.

And the Lord said to Moses, "Thou shalt do so." And Moses stretched forth his hand toward heaven, and the LORD caused hail to rain upon the land of Egypt. And God sent thunder and hail, and fire came down, which terrified the people, so they took it as a punishment from God. So there was hail and fire, and it was so severe that it had not been since it became a nation since they left Egypt.

And the hail struck throughout all the land of Egypt, both man and beast; and it became hail withal in all the land of Egypt. Where the children of Israel were, there was no hail. And Moses and Aaron had to come to Pharaoh and explain the plagues and that it was just an act of God, not theirs. Now please, Lord, I do not need any more of your thunder and lightning; I will let you go, and you will not come back.

And Moses said to Pharaoh, "Thus says the Lord, the God of the Hebrews: How long will you refuse to humble yourself before me? I want to make my people free. If you refuse my people to go, I will bring judgment into your country tomorrow. Locusts will cover the face of the earth so that no one can see the face of the earth. They will eat all of the leaves and all of the produce of the field, and they will even eat the last fruit of the trees. For your houses shall be filled with locusts, all your servants' houses, and the houses of all the Egyptians."

Pharaoh's men said to him, "How long will this man be a trap to us? Let the men go so that they may serve the Lord their God." Moses and Aaron were brought back to Pharaoh, and he asked them, "Who shall go?" "We will go with our young and old, our sons and daughters, with our flocks and herds, for we must hold a feast to the Lord." And He said, "The Lord will be with you if I let you and your little ones go. Watch out; your plan is evil. It won't happen! You ask them to go now, just the men and serve the Lord. And Pharaoh did not let them go. God said to Moses, "Stretch out your hand over the land of Egypt for the locusts, that they may come upon the land of Egypt, and eat everything the hail has left." And Moses stretched forth his rod over the land of Egypt. And the LORD set an east wind upon the land, and the east wind brought the locusts. With the appearance of these swarms of locusts, the situation was desperate, but there had never been such a swarm. Because they covered the face of the land, the land was destroyed.

The Lord told Moses, "Stretch out your hand toward heaven that there may be darkness over the land of Egypt." In Egypt, there was a heavy darkness that lasted for three days. There was no way for the people to communicate with each other.

None of the people were able to move during that time. It was very dark. And Pharaoh called for Moses and Aaron and said, "Go serve the Lord; just leave your sheep and your herds behind."

He commanded them to allow us to sacrifice and burn offerings to the Lord our God. We must take our cattle with us; not a bone is left behind. "For what we need to do, O Lord, will we not provide, but we know not what we will need until we get there." He hardened his heart, and he wouldn't let them go. And Pharaoh said to him, "You must never come back here again, for, on the day you return, you will be dead."

And then Moses and Aaron spoke to Pharaoh, saying, "This month will be the first month of your year." Speak to all the children of Israel; on the tenth day of this month, and each person shall offer a lamb. One must provide food for every family member, even if there are too few to feed. Your whole year shall be blessed. The scald shall be upon you on the 14th day of the month. And they shall destroy them at nightfall the entire congregation of the Israelites. Insert blood on the door frames, lintels, and the house where they are fed. The bread should be consumed with meat or poultry as long as it doesn't freeze. Do not eat it raw or cooked, but roast it: remove the head, and cook the insides. Burn everything except the rest of it. Thus shall you eat it: with your loins girded and in hand. It is the Lord's Supper. I will go throughout Egypt and strike down the firstborn in their houses. And thus shall I be seen to be the Lord. Also, you will see blood at the entrance doors. No worries. When I strike Egypt, there will be no plague upon you.

And he said to Moses and Aaron, "Go, you and the sons of Israel from among the people, and serve the Lord, as you have said." As I said, take your flocks and herds with you. Please bless me. In his yearning, the Egyptians cried, "Come out of the land swiftly, for we are all going to die." Then the people took out their dough before it was leavened, their kneading bowls behind their backs. And the children of Israel did according to the words of Moses, and they asked for articles of fine silvers and clothing. So the Lord let the people have what they asked for.

They swallowed the Egyptians. A total of more than six hundred thousand men and women were given into the hand of the Hebrews.

A mixed crowd also accompanied them; flocks and herds, with cattle in great numbers. They made unleavened bread from the dough that they had brought with them. Since they had not leavened it, they could not wait, so they did not have any provisions.

Now the time that the children of Israel dwelt in the land of Egypt was four hundred and thirty years. When this happened, on the day that all the hosts of the Lord left Egypt. This night is a most-honored night, which the Lord has commanded to be remembered, to be observed by all the children of Israel throughout their generations.

The Lord told Moses and Aaron that foreigners must not eat the Passover but that purchased male servants must be circumcised after the Passover is over, and then he must eat it. You are not allowed to take any part of it outside the house. The people of Israel shall celebrate it. If a stranger settles in with you and celebrates Passover, then all his males are to be circumcised. No uncircumcised person may eat of it.

Moses told the people, "Remember this day when you came out of Egypt. The Lord brought you out with a firm hand. You shall not eat leavened bread. When the Lord your God brings you to the land of the Canaanite, the Hittite, the Hivite, the Amorite, and the Jebusite, as he swore to your fathers, you shall set aside the first day of the seventh month for a sacred assembly. Seven days after, you shall eat unleavened bread, and on the 7th day, a feast to the Lord. You will eat seven unleavened bread for seven days, and no leavened bread will be seen on you in all your borders.

God led the people out of the wilderness by the Red Sea, and Israel went out of Egypt armed for battle. And Moses took the bones of Joseph with him, for he had solemnly sworn, "God will surely visit you, and you shall carry the bones away with you." They went out from Succoth and encamped on the outskirts of the wilderness. God carried them before the day with a pillar of cloud and by night with a pillar of fire so that they could see both day and night. The pillar of cloud by day and the pillar of fire by night did not depart from before the people.

So the Lord spoke to Moses, saying, "Tell the Israelites to turn back and camp before Pihahiroth, between Migdol and the sea. You will camp facing it by the sea. The Israelites will say to Pharaoh, "We have wandered away in the land, and the wilderness has blocked us in." And the Lord will make his heart stubborn, and he will pursue them and will honor my people and me, and the Egyptians will know that I am the Lord." And they did.

Then when the king of Egypt heard about what had happened, he changed his mind about the people and said, "What did we do, that we let Israel go from serving us?" He prepared his chariot and took six hundred of the best chariots of Egypt, all the chariots of Egypt, and officers over all of them.

The Lord hardened the heart of Pharaoh, king of Egypt, to prevent the children of Israel from going. The Egyptians pursued the horses and chariots of Pharaoh, his soldiers, and his cavalry and overtook them camping by the sea before Pihahiroth.

When Pharaoh approached, the children of Israel lifted their eyes and saw that the Egyptians were pursuing them. They were very afraid. And the Israelites cried out to the Lord. And the elders said to Moses, "Why did you take us out of Egypt to die in the wilderness? Why have you treated us in this way? Being sent ahead to deliver AryIans unto Egypt, saying, 'Leave us alone. We would have been better off if we had died in the wilderness." And Moses said to people: "Fear not and stand firm. See the salvation of the Lord today. For the Egyptians whom you have seen today, you will never see them again. God will fight for you, and you will be silent."

The Lord told Moses, "Why are you crying out to me?" Tell the Israelites to march forward. Lift up your rod and spread out your hand so that the children of Israel might walk on dry ground. I will harden the hearts of the Egyptians so that they will follow me. I will be honored above Pharaoh and all his army, chariots, and horsemen. And they will know that I am the Lord when I am respected in Egypt and on the chariots and horsemen.

God calmed the waters with a strong wind, dried them out all night, and turned the sea into dry land, and the waters were divided. And they went into the sea on dry ground. And they went into the sea on their right and on their left.

So Pharaoh's army pursued the Israelites and overtook them in the sea after they had swum. Then at the morning watch, God looked down on the Egyptian army through the pillar of fire and cloud and confused the army of the Egyptians. And he turned their camels' wheels into difficult paths. "We will do it (We will flee) because the Lord fights for them." Then God said to Moses, "You must stretch out your hand over the sea so that the waters may come back on the Egyptians." In the morning, the sea returned to normal. When the Egyptians saw this, they ran away.

Now, Jethro, the priest of Midian, heard all that God had done for Moses and Israel, how the Lord had brought Israel out of Egypt.

After he had sent her away, Moses' father-in-law took her and her two sons. One was Gershom, for he said, "I have been a sojourner in a foreign land"; the other was Eliezer, for the God of my father delivered me from the sword of Pharaoh." And Jethro, Moses' father-in-law, came with his sons and his wife to Moses in the wilderness where he was camping. And Jethro came and told Moses, "Your father-in-law is here and your wife and your two sons with her." After the meeting, Moses went out to meet his father-in-law, bowed, and kissed him. Then he brought them all into the tent. If you will listen, all that the Lord had done to Pharaoh and Egypt at their creation, their suffering on the way, and how he delivered them. The Lord was pleased with all the good things He had done for Israel in bringing them out of Egypt.

The laws

While in the desert, the third month after the children of Israel left Egypt, they arrived in the wilderness of Mount Sinai. Moses told the Elders what the Lord had told him to do and read the instructions to them. All the people said together, "We will obey whatever the LORD has spoken." And Moses reported the people's words to God. And the Lord said to Moses, "I am going to come to you in a thick cloud."

Then at daybreak the third day, there was an earthquake, and the mountain trembled violently, and a loud trumpet sounded, and all the people in the camp trembled. And Moses brought the people out of the camp and stood at the foot of the mountain. And Moses said to the Lord, "The people cannot come up to Mount Sinai; for you commanded us, saying, 'Make the mountain holy.'" Then the Lord said to him, "Go down and come up, and bring Aaron with you, but don't let the priests and the people go up with you lest he break out on them." Then Moses went down to the people and told them.

And God said all these words. I am the Lord, God of Israel, who freed you from the land of Egypt. I, the Lord your God, am a jealous God, visiting the iniquity of the fathers on the children, the third and fourth generation of those who hate me and showing loving kindness to thousands, to those who love me and keep my commandments. Everyone perceived the thunder and lightning and the sound of the trumpet. And when the people saw it, they trembled and stood at a distance.

These are the rules you shall set before them. If you buy a Hebrew servant, he will serve for six years and then be released. If he comes alone, he should go out alone; if he is married, his wife should go out with him. If he is married and she bears him sons or daughters, he will leave the household, and his wife and children will remain behind. If the employee plainly says, "I love my boss, my wife, and my kids; I will not leave a free man." then he will bring him to good, and he will bring him to the door. And his master will bring his ear through with an awl. And he will serve him forever.

If a man hits the eye of his slave and destroys it, he will let him go free as compensation. And if he knocks out the tooth of his male or female slave, he shall let him go free.

If an ox causes a man to die or a woman to become pregnant, the ox must be stoned. The owner of the ox shall not be held liable. If an ox is in the habit of goring, and the owner has been warned, but the ox kills a person, the ox will be stoned, and its owner will also be put to death.

If a man steals an ox or a sheep and slaughters it or sells it, he must pay five oxen for the ox and four sheep for a sheep. No bloodguiltiness attaches if he broke into a house and was struck or killed in the process. If the sun is up, the perpetrator must be held responsible. He shall pay restitution if he has anything. If he has not, he shall be sold for his theft. He shall pay two for one if the theft is found in his hand [alive], whether it be an ox, donkey, or sheep.

If a man defiles a virgin that is not engaged and lies with her, he shall surely be punished for her. If her father refuses to give her up, he must pay her father a dowry of virgins. You shall not allow a witch to live. Whoever is drunk shall be punished. He who sacrifices to other gods shall be destroyed, an eye for an eye.

Refrain from wrongdoing or oppression, for you were foreigners in Egypt. Leave windows and orphans alone. Also: Then you will suffer, and I will judge you with the sword, and you will die, and your children will become orphans. On the seventh day, you shall rest. No burden, no toil. Also, the weary traveler. That is all I've instructed you to do, and don't let them hear you say my own gods exist. A year has three months. At this time of the year, I tell you, eat unleavened red bread for seven days. And offer sacrifices. You will harvest the first fruits of your annual crops and gather them at the end of the year.

Set them apart to serve as priests. Harvest one ram that has no defects. Add refined wheat and unleavened dough. You are to grind them fine. Put them in the basket. You must wash Aaron and his two sons with water. Then you must get the tunic, the robe, the girdle, and the breastplate for him.

You will need to use an acacia plank of a length of 2 ft. and a half by 1 ft. The mold should be decorated with a gold mold. And light a lamp. The candlestick must be hand-forged and solid. Also, there will be four cups on the table.

The curtains will be 3' long, and the width of each curtain is four inches to separate the inside of the tent from the outside fully. You should take a blue cloth, scarlet material, and purple or purple cloth. Put it on four silver hooks and frames it on wooden staffs. You will weave a long purple and crimson curtain, and a spinner will make it. You are to use five braziers to make with gold and put a golden top on each of them.

Acacia wood should be used to build the altar. It should be four feet tall and three feet wide on all sides. You must also make a bronze cover for its four sides and a brass rim for its rim [part]. You must also make pots to remove its ashes, shovels, basins, flesh hooks, and fire pans. Gold, blue, purple, scarlet threads, and fine twined linen will be used to make the ephod. It should be made up of two shoulder pieces connected to one another. The girdle-like band on it, which is similar to its work, shall be made of gold, blue, purple, scarlet, and fine linen.

You must pay the Levites for each of the children of Israel when you take a census. That way, when you count them, there won't be any bald spots. After the sanctuary's shekel, each registered person must give half a shekel to the Lord. Everyone over the age of twenty-one is required to bring an offering to the Lord. Every priest requires a Shekel of gold, a quarter of a Shekel of silver, and a Shekel of copper, wood, or stone. And set aside a portion of the Levites' wages for the ministry. To make atonement for you, it will serve as a memorial for the tribe of Levi before the Lord.

The Lord spoke to Moses, saying, "See, I have called by name Bezalel, the son of Uri, the son of Hur, of the tribe of Judah; and I have filled him with the Spirit of God, in wisdom, in understanding, in knowledge, and all manner of workmanship, to devise skillful designs, to work in gold, silver, and bronze, in cutting stones for setting, and in carving wood, to work in all manner of craft. Look after [yourselves], take care of [yourselves], and each other. I have made you trustworthy and wise, so you can continue to observe all I have commanded. The tent of meeting, the Ark of the Covenant, the table and its utensils, the pure lampstand and its utensils, and the altar of incense are all included in the things I have made to be included in you.

Chapter 7

And Aaron said to them, "Take off the rings from your wives, your sons, and your daughters, and bring them to me." Everyone took off their gold rings, which were in their ears, and brought them to Aaron. He struck it, smelting it to metal, and then formed it into a molten calf. They said, "This is your god, Israel, the one who delivered you from Egypt." And Aaron built an altar before it and Aaron proclaimed, "Tomorrow will be a holy day." They rose early the next day, gave burnt offerings, and carried peace offerings. And the people sat down to eat and drink and rose up to play. And the Lord said to Moses, "I see these people. They are stubborn. Therefore leave me alone so that my anger burns hot against them, and I may destroy them. And I will turn you into a great nation." The Lord was very angry with Aaron and wanted to destroy him. Moses responded to the Lord: "Why does your anger burn against your people, who have been brought out of the land of Egypt with great power and with a mighty arm?"

Remember Abraham, Isaac, and Israel, your servants. They will have children as many as the stars of the sky, and I will give all this land that I have spoken of to your seed, and their descendants will inherit it forever. And the Lord relented the evil he had planned to do to his people. And Moses turned and walked down from the mountain with the two tablets of the Testimony in his hands. He carried them in his hands like tablets. The writing on the tablets was the work of God, and the writing was [the writing] of God. Then Joshua heard the people shouting and said to Moses, "There is a noise of war in the camp." And he said, "It is not the noise of victory, nor is it the sound of defeat. But the noise of singing I hear." Moses had a strong sense of anger and destroyed the tablets at the foot of the mountain. When Moses saw the people running wild, he stood at the camp gate and said, "Whoever is on the Lord's side, let him come to me." The children of Levi all gathered around him. And the Lord said to them, "Thus says the Lord: "Each man must have a sword on his thigh and go back and forth from place to place throughout the camp. Kill your brother, your companion, and your neighbor." And the sons of Levi did according to the word of Moses, and about 3,000 people fell that day. And Moses said, "Dedicate yourself today to the Lord. For every man has been against his son, and he may give a blessing on you today."

Chapter 8

God told Moses to cut two more tablets like the first. And present yourself to Mount Sinai. Beware, the mountain lest anyone approach or come with you." "Animals must not graze before the mountain." Live up to my expectations. May I be the first to drive out the Amorites, the Canaanites, the Jebusites, and the Girgas from before you? Pay attention lest you make a bargain with the inhabitants of the land you are crossing. So that you will lead away their sacred stones and demolitions and bear their pillars down, for them, so that you will not make a treaty with the Canaanites and then worship their pagan statues and their gods, and then make a treaty with them. You will eat their statues and their gods' idol "you shall not forge [your own] gods. It shall be in an unlined tunic. You shall eat unleavened bread all those days as I said, "All your male livestock is mine. And if you do not redeem the firstborn, you shall slay the lamb. Firstborn children are to be redeemed. None of them shall go away empty.

"You shall work six days, but on the seventh day, you shall rest; even in the time of the plowing and in the harvest, you shall rest. And thou shalt keep the feast of weeks, the first fruits of the harvest, and the feast of ingathering at the turn of the year. All your males shall appear three times a year before the Lord, the God of Israel. For I will cast out nations before you and enlarge [your boundary]; no one shall covet your land when you go up to appear before the Lord your God three times in the year."

And the Lord said to Moses, "Write these words, for I have made a covenant with you and with Israel according to these words." And he was there with the Lord forty days and forty nights; neither did he eat bread, nor drank water. And he wrote on the tablets the words of the covenant, the Ten Commandments.

And Moses did, setting forth all that the Lord entrusted him with. The tabernacle was set up on the first day of the second month in the first year that they came out of Egypt. And he erected its sockets, set up its hooks and its boards, put its bars in, and erected its pillars. And The Tent Was Put Over The Tabernacle, And He Put The Covering Of The Tabernacle Over It, As The Lord Commanded Moses.

And he took the testimony and put it within the ark, and [he set] the poles within the ark, and the mercy seat upon the ark. And He took the ark, and brought it into the tent, and set up the curtain for the ark of the testimony as God commanded to Moses. The table was put on the north side of the tent of meeting, on the outside of the veil.

LEVITICUS

"You shall be holy to me because I am holy." Lev 11:45 is the exemplary narrative of Leviticus. The book's name translates to "pertaining to the tribe of Levi," probably indicating that it was written for priests. It concerns laws that apply specifically to the sons of Levi and the sons of the high priest and what they must do to instruct the people of Israel. The book is short on plot but long on discussions about the law surrounding purity.

Chapter 1

Then the Lord spoke to Moses from the congregation and said, "Speak to the Israelites and say to them, if anyone presents an offering to the LORD, present it to God in the tent. It must be a burnt offering and be made according to the rules prescribed by God. The person who lays his or her hand on the sacrifice shall be redeemed. Also, he will kill the bull at the entrance to the tent, and the blood will be sprinkled around it. He shall slaughter the burnt-offering and cut off the feet. The priest's sons of Aaron shall set wood on the fire and set fire the fire.

In any sacrifice, one must also bring turtledoves or pigeons. Then the priest will take it and burn it outside the camp as a ritual purification and remove its head. It will be cut in half. It shall be consumed on the altar. It smells good to the Lord.

And when anyone offers his offering of grain to the Lord, his offering shall be of fine flour; and he shall pour oil on it, and put frankincense on it; it is a grain offering. And the priest shall take of his portion of the oil, the flour of the wave offering, and the wine-offering, and shall burn them on the altar, an offering made by fire of a sweet-smelling savor to the Lord. The grain offerings of fire will be Aaron's and his sons'. It is an extremely holy offering made by fire.

And if his offering is a sacrifice to the Lord of health, if it is a burnt offering from the herd, whether male or female, he shall offer it without blemish before the Lord. And he shall take his hand and kill it before the tent of meeting; then the sons of Aaron shall take the blood and sprinkle it around the altar.

Then you shall remove the fat that covers the kidneys and the fat on them. And he will remove the two kidneys by the loin and the fat upon them. Aaron's sons shall burn on the altar the fat of the burnt offering on the wood that is on the fire, an offering made by fire to the Lord.

Chapter 2

And the Lord spoke to Moses, saying, "Speak to the children of Israel, "If anyone accidentally does any of the things that the Lord has forbidden, and does any of them, then he shall die." If a priest with arthritis becomes ill and needs to be relieved of his responsibilities, he must bring a bull as a sin offering for the sin he committed. And he shall lead the bull to the tent of meeting's door, lay his hand on the bull's head, and slaughter the bull in front of the Lord. He then takes the bull's blood and transports it to the meeting tent. The priest will then dip his finger in the blood and sprinkle some of it before the Lord near the sanctuary's veil. If any of the common people unintentionally does any of the things the Lord has forbidden, and it is revealed to him, he must bring an unblemished female goat as an offering for his sin. And he is to kill the sin offering where the burnt offering is to be sacrificed. Some of its blood will be sprinkled on the altar's horns, while the rest will be poured out at the altar's base. "If anyone sins and steals or lies to his neighbor about a deposit or a pledge, or commits fraud, or finds that which is lost and lies about it, or swears falsely about it, in any of these ways that a man does, he shall restore what he stole or the thing he lied about, or the deposit or gift he was entrusted with, or the lost thing he found, if he has sinned and is guilty, he shall restore

He sanctified Aaron by pouring some of the oil on his head. As the Lord commanded Moses, Moses brought Aaron's sons and dressed them in tunics, sashes, belts, and headdresses.

The oil was poured on Aaron's head and anointed him to sanctify him. And Moses brought Aaron's sons to them dressed, and girded [them] with sashes, and bound [them] as the Lord commanded Moses. Then from the basket before the LORD, he took one unleavened cake, one loaf of bread mixed with oil, and one wafer and placed them on the fat and on the right thigh. He put them on Aaron's hands and on his sons' hands and waved them for a wave offering before the Lord. And Moses took them from their hands and burned them on the altar as a smell offering. It was a sacrificial smell offering.

And on the eighth day, Moses called Aaron and his sons and the elders of Israel; Aaron said, "Take two goats from the herd, a male without blemish and a ram without blemish, and offer them before the Lord." Say, "Please offer up a male lamb and a year-old calf without blemish for a burnt offering. Also, offer up an ox and a ram as an offering of well-being. And give as a grain offering a mixture of oil. Today the Lord shall appear to you." They brought the Ark of the Covenant. And all the people approached and stood before the Lord. Moses said, "This is the thing that the Lord commanded that you should do." And Moses said to Aaron, "Then come up to the altar and offer your sacrifice, and make atonement for yourself and the people, as the Lord commanded." Aaron approached the altar and slaughtered the calf on the altar. And the sons of Aaron presented it to him, and he touched with his finger the edge of the altar and poured out the blood at the base of the altar. And the fat of the sin offering, he burned upon the altar, as the Lord commanded Moses. And the flesh and the skin he burned outside the camp.

And he brought the burnt offering to the temple and sprinkled the blood around the altar. The burned offering was delivered piece by piece, and the head, which he burned on the altar. And he washed the entrails and the legs and burned them on the altar.

And, on each side, the censers were taken and were brought and put before the Lord, and incense was placed on them, and they did it, which the Lord had not prescribed to them. And there came forth a fire from before the Lord and consumed them. Then God said, "I will be glorified through those who approach me, and I will be sanctified through all of the people." And Aaron was silent.

And the Lord said to Aaron: "Do not drink any wine or strong drink, neither you nor your sons with you when you go into the tent of meeting that you might not die. It shall be a statute forever throughout your generations, and you may teach the children of Israel all the statutes the Lord has spoken to them by Moses." And Moses spoke to Aaron, Eleazar, and Ithamar, his sons that were left, "Take the grain that remains of the offerings of the Lord, made by fire, and eat it in a holy place, because it is your portion and your sons' portion, of the offerings of the Lord, made by fire; for so I am commanding you."

You shall eat the breast and thigh of the wave offering and the thigh of the heave offering that is given as your portion, from the portion of your sons and daughters, from the sacrifices of the Lord's peace offerings. You shall take a portion from the ram and the male goat as a wave offering and shall wave it before the Lord, a memorial for you; and it shall be yours and your sons' forever, as the Lord has commanded.

When Moses was looking for the sin offering, he found it had been burned. He was angry with Eleazar and Ithamar, the sons of Aaron. Moses said, "Why have you not eaten the sin offering in the sanctuary? It is most holy. I gave it to you to bear the iniquity of the congregation, to make atonement for them before the Lord." "Look here; you should certainly have eaten it in the sanctuary, as I commanded." ("And Aaron spoke to Moses: "Here today, they have offered their sacrifices before the Lord. As things like this happen to me, if I had eaten the sacrifice today, would it have been pleasing to the Lord?") And when Moses heard this, he was pleased.

God spoke to Moses after the death of the two sons of Aaron and said to Moses, "Speak to Aaron your brother, and tell him not to enter the Holy of Holies within the veil, before the mercy seat which is on the ark, that he not die, for I will appear in the cloud on the mercy seat."

He shall then come into the sanctuary with a young bull and a ram for a burnt offering. He shall wear the holy linen tunic next to his body, with the linen undergarments on top, and shall be girded with the linen sash, which are the holy garments. And he shall bathe his flesh and put them on. In the desert shall he bring forth his burnt offering, of one ewe lamb, and one ram, for a sin offering.

Aaron shall take the bull, the sin offering for himself, and make atonement for himself and his house. Then the priest shall kill the goat for the people and bring its blood inside the veil, smear its blood on the mercy seat, and sprinkle the blood of the sin offering before the mercy seat. He shall make atonement for the holy place since the filthiness of the Israelites and the evil of their acts. He shall also make atonement for the Tent of Meeting because of their [sin, evil deeds].

"Speak to all the congregation of the children of Israel and say to them 'You shall be holy, for I, the Lord your God, am holy.'" You shall respect your parents, and you shall keep my Sabbaths. I am the Lord your God. Do not make any idols for yourselves; I am the Lord your God.

"When you offer a sacrifice for your well-being to the Lord, you may be accepted. It must be eaten within two days of making it or on the third day; if anything is left, it must be burned. If it is eaten on the third day, it is forbidden. It cannot be accepted. Everyone who eats it is to bear his iniquity because he has profaned the holy thing of the Lord. To keep my Sabbaths and respect my sanctuary, I am the Lord.

Do not seek mediums or wizards, so they will not defile you; I am the Lord your God. "You shall rise up before the aged and honor the old. Fear your God. I am the Lord." "You should not wrong a foreigner who resides with you in your land." The native among you shall be your friend and the stranger shall love you as your own. You shall not do unrighteousness in terms of longitude, weight, or the amount; square measures, 60 cubits, is the just measure; I am the Lord your God who brought you out of the land of Egypt. I have commanded you to observe all my statutes and obey them. I am the Lord.

When the priest has finished consecrating your father's house, you will complete the task in the same manner. And if the person is willing to pay the total amount, he can redeem his house. Dedicating a field to the Lord requires putting in the proper effort. That'll make three-homer bars of silver. If he builds it from there on, it will remain. And then, when he has completed the dedication of his offerings to the Lord, he shall return and settle his account. If the individual who bought the field wants to redeem it, he must return 1/5 of the money. It can no longer be redeemed if he does not save the land. The land will be released in the jubilee will be hallowed. It will belong to the priest. If he sells it to a foreigner, it belongs to the foreigner. The whole land belongs to God." The Lord is pleased. He may donate as much as he likes."

NUMBERS

This book begins with the Israelites in the Sinai desert, covers their forty years of wandering, and ends with the people ready to cross the Jordan River into the Promised Land. Our English title comes from the Greek title Arithmoi, perhaps chosen because Numbers opens with a census. However, the Hebrew title Bemidbar, meaning "In the Desert," seems more appropriate to the book's central theme.

Chapter 1

And on the first day of the second month, the Lord spake unto Moses in the Tabernacle of the Congregation, saying, 'Sum up the children of the people according to their families, by their fathers' every male, every male, and every woman child, by their names; and there shall be with you representatives of every tribe, a man from the house of the leader of the families. And these are the people who are supporting you.

To Reuben, his son: The tribe of Reuben had a total of 46,500 men. Of the descendants of Simeon, every generation, starting with those who were twenty and up, were prepared to participate in the conflict. Of all the generations of Benjamin, theirs by their house, and by age, from twenty up, numbered; their descendants numbered 35,400. Among the two thousand Danites, the total of all the families were sixty-two thousand and seven hundred. The descendants of Asher's, both by their fathers' houses and by their names, from twenty and upwards who were able to go to war.

For the Lord has spoken to Moses, saying, "Only the tribe of Levi shall you be numbered, nor shall you be numbered among the Israelites; but the Levites shall be numbered over the tabernacle of the testimony, and over all its furniture; and they shall bear the tabernacle, and all its furniture; and they shall take care of it, and encamp around the tabernacle.

These are the names of the sons of Aaron, of the anointed priests, of whom they have been ordained to serve the priesthood. But Nadab and Abihu died before the Lord when they offered illicit fire before the Lord in the wilderness of Sinai. They had no children, so Eleazar and Ithamar served in the priest's office during the lifetime of their father, Aaron.

And the Lord spoke unto Moses, saying, "Bring the tribe of Levi near and set them before Aaron, the priest, that they may minister unto him. And they shall perform their duties for him, and the entire congregation before the tabernacle of meeting, to do the service of the tabernacle. And they shall take care of all the furniture of the tabernacle of the congregation, and the duties of the children of Israel, as they serve in the tabernacle. And thou shalt give the Levites unto Aaron and his sons: they shall be wholly given unto him from among the children of Israel. You shall appoint Aaron and his sons, and they shall attend to their priesthood, but every layman who comes near shall be put to death." And the Lord spoke unto Moses, and said, "Behold, I have taken the Levites from among the children of Israel, instead of every firstborn that openeth the womb, from among the children of Israel. The Levites shall be mine; for all the firstborn are mine; on the day that I slew all the firstborn in the land of Egypt, I consecrated the firstborn in Israel, both man and beast; I am the Lord."

Then the Lord spoke to Moses and Aaron, saying, "Take a census of the sons of Kohath from among the sons of Levi, from their families and their fathers' houses, from thirty years old and up to sixty years old, all who are able to enter the service, to work in the tent of meeting. This is the service of the sons of Kohath in the tent of meeting concerning the holiest things. When the camp is set up, Aaron and his sons shall go in, and they shall take down the veil of the [screen] and the ark of the testimony with it; and they shall put a covering of the seal on it, and sprinkle a cloth of pure blue over it, and put it on the poles.

Thus, the Lord spoke to Moses, "Command the Israelites to expel every leper and every unclean person who has had come into contact with a corpse that they may not defile it." Thus, and so, and Israel sent them out, the words of Moses were as the Lord had instructed.

So, then the Lord spoke to Moses, saying, "Speaking to the Israelites: A man or a woman who commits a sin that is one of the people, and does that sin, is guilty and must admit guilt, and pay back the fivefold, and also make restitution to the one they wronged." If there is no relative to whom the debt may be repaid, the debt of innocence is repaid to God.

And all of Israel's offerings to the priest shall be considered holy. This was the dedication offering for the altar from the leaders of Israel on the day it was anointed: twelve silver plates and all the oxen for peace offerings, twenty-four bulls, sixty rams, sixty male goats, and sixty male lambs a year old. The altar was dedicated after it had been anointed.

Thus you shall do to them, to cleanse them: to sprinkle on them the water of purification, to shave their whole body with a razor, and to wash their clothes, and to purify themselves. Then let them take a young bull and its grain offering of fine flour mixed with oil and take another young bull for a sin offering. And ye shall bring the Levites before the tabernacle of the congregation and gather the whole community of the children of Israel. When you bring the Levites before Yahweh, the Israelites shall lay their hands on the Levites; and Aaron shall offer the Levites before Yahweh as a wave offering from the Israelites, that it may be theirs to do the service of Yahweh.

Then Miriam and Aaron spoke against Moses [because of the Cushite woman whom he had married], because [he had married] a Cushite woman. And they said, "Has the Lord spoken only through Moses? Has he not spoken through us, too?" And the Lord had heard it. Now Moses was a man who was more humble than all the people who were on the face of the earth. And the Lord spoke suddenly to Moses, Aaron, and Miriam, "Come out, you three, to the Tent of Meeting." And the Lord came down in a pillar of cloud, and stood at the door of the tabernacle, and called Aaron and Miriam, and they came forward. And the Lord said to them, "Hear now My words: if there is a prophet among you, I, the Lord, will make myself known to him in a vision; I will speak to him in a dream. Not so with my servant Moses; he is faithful in all my house. And not in the dark, but the form of the Lord; and he hath seen the form of the Lord. Why then were you not afraid to speak against Moses, against my servant?" And the anger of the Lord was kindled against them, and he departed. And the Lord spoke to them, and Aaron, saying, "This is the statute of the law which the Lord commanded, saying, 'Tell the Israelites to bring you a heifer [unblemished red], in which there is no defect, and on which no yoke has been laid. And you shall give it to Elea, the priest, and they shall bring it out of the camp and kill it for him.

Then Elea the priest shall take some of the blood with his finger and sprinkle some of the blood toward the door of the tent of meeting seven times. Then shall the heifer burnt in his sight; his skin, and his flesh, and his blood, and his dung, shall he burn. And the priest shall take cedar wood, hyssop, and scarlet and cast them in the midst of the burning heifer." And the Lord spake unto Moses, saying, "Take the rod, and gather the congregation, thou, and Aaron, thy brother, and command the rock before their eyes to bring forth its water. You shall bring for them water out of the rock, and you shall give them drink for the congregation and their cattle."

They began their journey in Kadesh and traveled all the way to Mount Hor. "Aaron shall be gathered unto his people," the Lord told Moses and Aaron at Mount Hor on the Edom border. Because you disobeyed my command at the waters of Meribah, he shall not enter the land that I have given to the people of Israel. Bring Aaron and Eleazar up to Mount Hor with you. And you are to take Aaron's clothes off and put them on Eleazar. Aaron will be returned to his people, where he will die."

They went up Mount Hor, as the Lord had commanded, in front of the entire congregation. Aaron was then stripped naked and placed on his son, Eleazar. Aaron died at the summit of the mountain. After that, Moses and Eleazar descended the mountain. When the congregation learned of Aaron's death, they mourned for him for thirty days.

These are the names of the men Moses dispatched to scout the area. Hoshea, the son of Nun, was renamed Joshua by Moses. Moses then sent them out to scout the land of Canaan, telling them, "Go up into the Negev, and up into the hill country, and see what the land is like and whether the people who live there are strong or weak; few or many; and whether the land [in which they live] is good or bad; and whether the cities in which they live are as camels? And be bold, and bring [some of] the land's fruit back with you." It was now time for the first season of ripe [grapes].

And they went up, went in, and spied out the land from the wilderness of Zin to Rehob, at the entrance of Hamath. And they went up through the Negev and came to Hebron; Ahaiman, Sheshai, and Tolmai, the descendants of Anak, were there.

Now Hebron had been built [seven years] before Zoan in Egypt. And they came to the valley of Eshcol, and cut down from there a branch with a cluster of grapes, carried it on a pole between them, and brought in some pomegranates and figs. It was called the valley of Eshcol because of the cluster the Israelites had cut off from.

Arad, the Canaanite king, took some captive when he heard that Israel had advanced down the road to Atharim. He vowed to the Lord, saying, "I will totally destroy their cities."

And the Lord started to Moses, "Do not attack or molest Moab, for I have given it to the sons of Lot." And the Lord spoke to Moses, saying, "today you will come near the Ammonites, and I will not give them any of the lands of the Ammonites to inherit, since I have given it to the descendants of Lot, who dwell in the wilderness as their possession.'"

So the elders of Moab and the elders of Midian departed with the divination charges in their hand, and they came to Balaam and repeated to him the words of Balak. He said to them, "Stay here tonight, and I will bring back word to you, just as the Lord speaks to me." So the leaders of Moab remained with Balaam.

And God came to Balaam and said to him, "Who are these men with you?" And Balaam said to God, Balak the son of Zippor, king of Moab, has sent a message to me, 'See, this people has come out of Egypt, and they cover the face of the earth, and they are living near me. Now, curse them for me; I may be able to fight against them and drive them out of the land. And God said to Balaam, "Do not go to the men, and do not go to the people, for they are blessed." So Balaam rose up in the morning and said to the leaders of Balaam, "Go back to your lord, for the Lord has refused to let me go with you." The leaders of Moab rose and went to Balak and said to him, "Balaam refuses to come with us."

And Balaam said to Balak, "Build seven altars for me here, and prepare seven bulls and seven rams for me." And Balak did as Balaam had said, and Balak and Balaam offered a ram on each altar. Then Balaam said to Balak, "Stand with your burnt offering, and I will go; maybe God will come to meet me, and whatever he may show me, I will tell you."

55

And Balak went and stood by his offering, and Balaam called to God and went to a barren height. The angel of God met Balaam and said, "I have prepared the seven altars, and I have offered on each altar a bull and a ram." Then the Lord put a word in Balaam's mouth and said, "Return to Balak, and you shall speak this way." So he returned to him, and he stood beside his burnt offering and all the rulers of Moab. Then Balak said to Balaam, "Please come with me to another place, from where you may see them; you shall see only a part of them, and you shall not see them all then curse them for me from there." Then Balak took him to the field of Zophim, to the top of Pisgah, built seven altars, and offered a bull and a ram on each altar.

And when Balaam saw that it pleased the Lord to bless Israel, he went not as at other times, to look for the omens, but set his face toward the wilderness. And Balaam lifted up his eyes and saw Israel encamped by the tribe. And the Spirit of God came upon him, and uttered his oracle, and said The oracle of Balaam the son of Beor, and the oracle of the man whose eye is opened; the oracle of him that heareth the words of God that seeth the vision of the Almighty, that falleth, and hath uncovered his eyes. How fair are your tents, O Jacob, your tents, O Israel! Like valleys stretching out, like gardens beside a river, like tents set up by the Lord, like cedar trees beside the waters.

Water shall flow out of his buckets, his seed shall be many waters, his king shall be higher than Agag, and his kingdom shall be exalted. God, who brings him out of Egypt, is like a wild ox's horns; he shall devour the nations that are his adversaries, break their bones in pieces, and smite them with his arrows. He is ugly; he stretches out like a lion and like a lion who dares to rouse him? Blessed are those who bless you, and cursed are those who curse you."

Balak's anger was kindled against Balaam, and he clapped his hands together. And Balak said to Balaam, "I have called you to curse my enemies, but behold, you have blessed them these three times. And it came about after the plague that the Lord spoke to Moses and Eleazar, son of Aaron the priest, saying, "Take a census of all the congregation of the Israelites, from twenty years old and upward, by their fathers' houses, all in Israel who are able to go out to war."

and said to Moses and Eleazar the priest in the desert near the Jordan, "Count all the people, from 20 years old and upward as Moses had ordered"

Now the Israelites who came out of the land of Egypt were: Reuben, the firstborn of Israel, the descendants of Reuben: of Hanoch, the clan of the Hanochites; of Pallu, the clan of the Palluites; of Hezron, the clan of the Hezronites; of Carmi, the clan of the Carmelites. These are the Reubenites, which number is forty-three thousand and thirty-seven.

Pallu and his descendants' Children of Eliab: Nemuel and Abiam. These are the Dathan and Abiram who were chosen from the congregation, who, along with Koraanai, revolted against Moses and the Lord, who were killed. At the same time, the fire consumed two hundred fifty and fifty men who burned offering incense. Afterward, the fire swallowed them and killed the other two hundred and fifty.

The descendants of Simeon according to their clans: of Nemuel, the clan of the Nemuelites; of Jamin, the clan of the Jaminites; of Jachin, the clan of the Jachinites; of Zerah, the clan of the Zerahites; of Shaul, the clan of the Shaulites.

These are the clans of the Simeonites: twenty-two thousand two hundred. The descendants of Gad: Zephon, the clan of Zephonites; the clans of Shuni, the Shunites, and the clans of Erites. According to those who were numbered, these are the clans of the sons of Gad: forty thousand five hundred. The sons of Judah: Er and Onan; Er and Onan died in the land of Canaan. And the descendants of Judah by their clans were: of Shelah, the clan of the Shelanites; of Perez, the clan of the Perezites; of Zerah, the clan of the Zerahites. And Perez's descendants were: Hezron, the clan of the Hezronites; Hamul, the clan of the Hamuelites. These are the clans of Judah according to those that were numbered of them: seventy-three thousand five hundred. The descendants of Issachar according to their clans: of Tola, the clan of the Tolaites; of Puvah, the clan of the Puvites; of Jashub, the clan of the Jashubites; of Shimron, the clan of the Shimronites. These are the clans of Issachar, according to those who were numbered of them: sixty-four thousand three hundred.

The descendants of Zebulun by their clans: Sered, the clan of the Series; Elon, the clan of the Elonites; Jahleel, the clan of the Jahleelites. These are the clans of the Zebulunites, according to those numbered sixty thousand and five hundred. The descendants of Joseph, according to their clans: Manasseh and Ephraim. The descendants of Manasseh: Machir, the clan of Machir, and Machir, the father of Gilead; Gilead, the clan of the Gileadites.

These are the descendants of Gilead: of Ahiezer, the clan of the Ahiezerites; of Helek, the clan of the Helekites; and of Asriel, the clan of the Israelites; and of Shechem, the clan of the Shechemites; and of Shemida, the clan of the Shemidites; and of Hepher, the clan of the Hopherites. Now Zelophehad, the son of Hepher had no sons but daughters, and these are the names of the daughters of Zelophehad: Mahlah, Noah, Hoglah, Milcah, and Tirzah. These are the clans of Manasseh, of whom fifty-two thousand and seven hundred were numbered.

And the Lord said to Moses, "Go up to this mountain of Abarim and see the land which I have given to the people of Israel. And it shall come to pass, when you have seen it, that you also shall be gathered to your people, as Aaron your brother was gathered together." And the Lord said to Moses, "Take Joshua the son of Nun, a man in whom is the spirit, and lay your hand on him; and let him stand before Eleazar, the priest, and before all the congregation, and command him in their sight. You shall give him some of your authority, that all the congregation of the children of Israel may obey him. But he shall stand before Eleazar the priest, who shall inquire of him by the decision of the Urim before the Lord: at his word shall they go out, and at his word shall they come in, he and all the Israelites with him, the whole congregation with him."

Here is the Lord's instruction for you: A man sticks to his word and fulfills his commitment. The promises a young woman made while in her father's house are as strong as steel. But if her father doesn't allow it, neither will her oaths. If she is married, then her thoughts and statements will be taken by her husband, and if she is silent about it, her vows remain intact. But, on that day, He will allow her to be set free.

He validates all of her vows if he never speaks to her. However, he will suffer the consequences. These are the laws that the godless statues of Moses found to be in a son-in-in-law and his father-in-in-house. law's

Follow the Lord's instructions while traveling out of the land of Egypt. Moses listed their starting points according to the guidelines that were provided. They departed from Rameses on the fifteenth day of the first month and marched into the view of all the Egyptians. The gods were overthrown. They camped in Succoth. They set out from Succoth and camped at Etham. They set out from Etham and returned to Pi-hirath. They left Hahiroth and went on for three days in the Megiddo Desert. Finally, Elim is home of twelve springs and seventy-plus date trees.

They set out from Risha and went to Keshet. They left Kehelath and headed for Mount Shepher. In Harad, they set out, and they camped there. They left Harad and camped at Mako'tô. From Makoroth and Tahatt. And they left Tahat and camped at Terah, and they camped at Mishteeath. From there, they set up camp at Hashmonah. And they camped at Moseroth. They left Moseroth and pitched camp in E'bonka. From Bene-Anak, they set out and encamped in Hor-had. And they camped at Hor and settled in Joshimath. And departed from Abronah.

They departed from Iim and camped there. They set off from Dibon and camped in Almoniblah. Finally, they set out from Almon and camped in the land of Abarim. So they departed from the heights of Mount Abarim and camped by the River Jordan. Then they camped along the banks of the Jordan by Abel- well.

And God said to the Israelites, '"when you enter the land of Canaan, you must drive out the people who dwell there and demolish all their engraved stones and demolish their statuettes' so that you may have it. And you shall divide the land according to your clans. Regardless of who dies, every one shall receive according to the tribe of his fathers."

Tell the Israelites, "Enter the land of Canaan'" Your southern sector runs from the wilderness of Zin to the edge of the Sea of Edom on the east, and goes down to the Wilderness of Arabia to the south of Kadeshbarnea, then it hits the coast of the Dead Sea of Arabia, then to the Wilderness of

Israel, which is the south of Hazar, and then finally ends in the salt water of the Dead Sea of the Sea of Egypt.

This shall be your western boundary. Including the Great Sea to Hor, from there, and out to Zedad, and Hazarim to Siphon, and ending with that shall be your northern limit: it shall be your limit.

And the towns shall be theirs to live in, and their land will be for livestock. All their animals and to the outer perimeter of the city, which you shall allot to the tribe of the Levites And you shall measure two thousand cubits on the east side of the city, and two thousand cubits on the south side, and two thousand cubits on the west side, and two thousand cubits on the north side; and the city shall be in the middle. It will serve as lands for their cities.

"Speak to the Israelites, and say to them, 'When you cross the Jordan into the land of Canaan, then you shall choose cities for yourselves as cities of refuge for you, so that the manslayer who killed any person without purpose may flee there. Your enemies will not kill you until the courts have their way with you. And the six cities you shall be your hiding places. Designate three locations beyond the Jordan and three in the land of Canaan; they shall be refuge cities. For the Israelites, and for the stranger, and for the sojourner among them, these six cities shall be for refuge, that whoever kills an unintentional person may flee there.

DEUTERONOMY

Moses is the main character in this book, referenced from when the Israelites left Sinai to the burial of their great leader. Since Deuteronomy also includes the authoritative law given to Israel by God through Moses, it is the only Pentateuch book that explicitly identifies itself as a record of the laws of Moses.

Chapter 1

These are the words that Moses spoke to all of Israel in the wilderness across the Jordan, in the Arabah opposite Suph, between Paran, Tophel, Laban, Hazeroth, and Di-zahab, in the Arabah between Paran, Tophel, Laban, Hazeroth, and Di-zahab. Horeb to Mount Seir to Kadesh-Barnea is an eleven-day journey. After he had defeated Sihon king of the Amorites, who dwelt in Heshbon, and Og king of Bashan, who dwelt in Ashtaroth, in Edrei, in the forty-first year, in the eleventh month, on the first day of the month, Moses spoke to the children of Israel, according to all that the Lord had commanded him concerning them. "The Lord, our God, spoke to us in Horeb, saying, 'You have stayed long enough in this mountain; turn and take your journey, and go to the hill country of the Amorites, and to all their neighbors in the Arabah, in the hill country, and in the lowland, in the Negev, and by the sea, the land of Canaan," Moses began to explain this law. See, I have prepared the land for you; enter and occupy the land that the Lord promised to your forefathers, Abraham, Isaac, and Jacob, and to their descendants after them.

Then Moses called all of Israel and said to them, "So listen! I am instructing you about the statutes and rules that I am speaking to you today so that you will be able to follow them, so that you will remember them and carry them out: God our Father established a covenant with us in Horeb. This agreement was not given to our ancestors but to all of us who are alive today. The Lord talked to you face to face while on top of the mountain.

But while was standing between you and the Lord, speaking to you on His holy mountain, He saved you. And he remarked:

"I am the Lord your God who brought you out of the land of Egypt, out of the house of bondage." You shall have no gods before me."

You may not make an image of any entity that exists in the heavens nor the depths of the sea. You shall not bow down to them, nor serve them for I, the Lord your God will visit the sins on your children, from generation to generation to show mercy to thousands of those who obey Me and to their children." You shall not speak slanderously of the name of the Lord his God.

Seek the LORD your God's command on the seventh day," And in the seventh, you must do your own work." Do not hire your son, your female servant, your ox, or your stranger in your town's entrance to keep your female servant safe. The Lord, your God, brought you out with a firm hand and a great effort. Hence, God, therefore, ordered you to respect it Thus God created the heavens.

Honor thy father and thy mother, as the Lord thy God hath commanded thee, that thy days may be long, and that it may be well with thee in the land which the Lord thy God hath given unto thee. You are not going to commit murder. You must not commit adultery. You're not going to steal. You shall not bear false witness to your neighbor.

You shall not covet your neighbor's wife; you shall not covet the house of your neighbor, his field, his male servant, his female servant, his ox, his ass, or anything that belongs to your neighbor. These are the words which the Lord spoke to your entire congregation on the mountain from the midst of the fire, the darkness, the cloud, and the thick darkness, with a great voice, and he added no more. Then he wrote them down on two stone tablets and gave them to me.

When you heard the voice from the midst of the darkness while the mountain burned with fire, you came near to me, all the heads of your tribes and your elders. And you said, "Behold, the Lord our God has shown us his glory and his greatness, and we have heard his voice out of the midst of the fire; and we have seen in this day that the Lord speaks to men, and they live. So now, why are we supposed to die? For this great fire shall consume us; if we continue to hear the voice of the Lord our God, we shall die."

This is the commandment, the statutes, and the ordinances which the Lord your God commanded me to teach you so that you might observe them in the land where you are living. Pay attention, therefore, to this, and make it succeed in your body and mind, just as the Lord, your God, the God of your ancestors, has promised, as you enter a land flowing with milk and honey.

Hear, O Israel, Jehovah our God, Jehovah is one; and thou shalt love Jehovah thy God with all thy heart, and with all thy soul, and with all thy might. And these words, which I command you today, shall be in your hearts. You shall teach them diligently to your children and speak of them when you sit in your house, and when you walk along the road, and when you lie down, and when you rise up. And you shall bind them on your hand as a sign, and they shall be for frontlets between your eyes. And you will write them on the doorposts of your house and on your doorstep. When the Lord your God brings you into the land which he swore to your ancestors, to Abraham, to Isaac, and to Jacob, to give you—a land of great and fine cities that you did not build, houses full of all the good things that you did not fill, hewn cisterns that you did not dig, vineyards and olive trees that you did not plant when you ate and were satisfied, be careful not to forget.

And thou shalt keep the commandments of the Lord thy God, walking in all his ways, and loving him. For the Lord your God is bringing you into a good and spacious land—a land of brooks of water, fountains, and springs, flowing out into valleys and hills; a land of wheat and barley, vineyards, fig trees and pomegranates; a land of olive oil and honey; a land where you shall eat bread without scarcity, and where you shall lack nothing; a land whose stones are iron, and from whose hills you shall come.

Bless and be thankful for the good land which He has given you. Follow the instructions I've given you today. Otherwise, when you are content and have acquired wealth, your flocks and herds will grow, and the Lord will be absent from your heart. In the middle of an arid region, a desolate place, He provided manna for your ancestors; at the end of the ages, He provided water from a stone for you. However, you know you deserve it because you've worked hard for it. Thus, keep in mind that your forebears have given you the ability to succeed.

And the LORD said to me, "Go up to the mountain, and build two stone tablets." These will be inscribed on the tablets of the Lord's covenant. So I constructed an acacia ark and set out with the two tablets in hand. Then the Lord spoke to you, and I handed them to him. And there I was, just as the Lord had told me to do. So the Israelites set out for Madmenah. Eleazar, Aaron's only son, was buried. His son filled his shoes. They went to Gomray and Gogmagogmagog. At that time, the tribe of Levi was established, and they serve until the coming of the Lord. Thus, Levi is without a claim or entitlement to any inheritance. For 40 days and nights, the Lord didn't allow you to die. Then the Lord spoke to me, saying, "Go ahead of the people and the nations, and My land will be given to you."

These are the commandments the Lord has set before you for the land which your forefathers, the God of your fathers, have given you.

Ye shall surely destroy all the places where the nations whom ye dispossessed have served their gods: upon the high mountains, hills, and under every green tree. And thou shalt break down their altars, and break their pillars in pieces, and burn their Asherim with fire, and thou shalt cut down the graven images of their gods, and thou shalt cut off their name from that place. You shall not do this to the Lord your God. But you shall seek the place which the Lord your God shall choose out of all your tribes, to put his name there for his dwelling, and there you shall go.

Then you shall bring everything to the place to which the Lord decides to put his name: your burnt offerings, your contributions, your donations, and your promises to the Lord. Additionally, you shall rejoice before the Lord your God: you, your male servants, your female servants, and the Levite within your gates.

If there arises in your midst a prophet or a dreamer, and he gives you a sign or a wonder, and if there is a sign or a wonder about which he has spoken to you; and if he says, "Let us go after other gods—which you have not known—and let us serve them," you shall not listen to the words of that prophet or dreamer. The Lord is testing you to see if you love the Lord your God with all your heart and your soul. Fear the Lord your God, serve him, adhere to his will, and heed his commands.

And that prophet, or dreamer of dreams, shall be put to death, because he hath spoken rebellion against the Lord your God, who brought you out of the land of Egypt and redeemed you out of the house of bondage, by taking you aside from the way in which the Lord your God commanded you to walk. So you're going to purge the evil from your midst.

If your neighbor—whether the son of your father, or the son of your mother, or your son, or the wife whom you cherish, or your friend who is nearest to you—conveys you secretly, saying, "Let us go and serve other gods,"—the gods of the peoples who are around you, near you, or far from you, from the ends of the earth to the other ends of the earth.

Your eye will not pity or shield him or spare him, but you must surely put him to death. Your hand is first upon him to put him to death and then upon the hands of all the people.

You shall stone him to death with stones because he has sought to draw you from the Lord your God, who brought you out of the land of Egypt, out of the house of bondage. Then all Israel will hear and be afraid, and they will no longer do the evil that is in your midst.

You are the sons of the Lord your God. You shall not cut yourselves nor shave your forehead to the dead. For you are a holy people to Yahweh your God, and Yahweh has chosen you to be a person for his own possession, above all the nations that are on the face of the earth. You shall not eat anything abominable. You can eat these beasts: the ox, the sheep, and the goat.

And all winged creeping things are unclean to you; you shall not eat of them. You can eat of all the clean birds. You shall not eat anything that dies by itself. [You may give it] to the stranger who is within your gates, that he may eat it, or that you may sell it to a stranger; for you are holy to the Lord your God. You shall not boil a kid in the milk of his mother.

You shall tithe all the increase of your seed from the field year by year. Eat the tithe of your crops, the firstling of your cattle, and then of your sheep, in the presence of the Lord your God, so that you may always revere the Lord. But if the road is too long for you, so that you cannot carry the tithe, because the place is too far away from you, where the Lord your God chooses to set his name, when the Lord your God blesses you, then you shall exchange it for money, bind the money in your hand, and go to the place which the Lord your God chooses. You may spend the money on oxen, wine, or strong drink, or any other intoxicant you desire." You shall eat there before the Lord your God and rejoice over you and your household. And as for the Levite who is within your gates, you shall not neglect him, for he has no portion or inheritance with you.

You shall grant a remission of debts at the end of every seven years. And this is the way of remission: every creditor shall release what he has lent to his neighbor; he shall not exact 100 because the remission of the Lord has been proclaimed. You may be able to tell the foreigner, but whatever of yours is with your brother, your hand will be handed over.

But there shall be no poor among you; for the Lord will surely bless you in the land which the Lord your God gives you for an inheritance to possess, if only you will fully hear the voice of the Lord your God, to keep this entire commandment which I command you this day. For the Lord your God will bless you, as he promised you; you will lend to many nations, but you will not borrow; you will rule over many nations, but they will not rule over you.

Do not be hardhearted or tight-fisted toward your poor neighbor if there is anyone in need among you—a member of your community in any of your towns within the land that the Lord your God is giving you. Instead, you will open your hand to him and lend him enough to meet his needs, whatever he may require. Be careful that there is no evil thought in your heart that says, "The seventh year, the year of remission, is at hand," and that your eye is hostile to your needy neighbor, and you don't give him anything. Then he may cry out [to the Lord, against you], and it shall be accounted to you as a sin. Thou shalt indeed give unto him, and thy heart shall not be grieved when thou shalt give unto him: therefore the Lord thy God shall bless thee in all thy work, and in all that thou shalt put thy hand upon.

Keep the Passover for the Lord your God in the month of Abib because it was in this month that the Lord your God brought you out of Egypt by night. And you shall sacrifice the Passover to the Lord your God from your flock and herd in the place where the Lord has chosen to put his name. You shall not eat leavened bread with it for seven days; instead, you shall eat unleavened bread, the bread of affliction, since you fled Egypt in haste—so that you may remember the day you fled the land of Egypt all your days.

And for seven days, no leaven shall be seen with you in all your borders nor shall any of the meat that you sacrifice on the first day's evening remain all night until the morning.

You may not offer the Passover sacrifice in any of the towns that the Lord your God has given you, but only in the place where the Lord your God has chosen to make his name dwell. You must sacrifice the Passover there in the evening, when the sun sets, at the time when you left Egypt.

Then you shall cook it and eat it in the place that the Lord your God chooses for you, and you shall return to your tents in the morning. You must eat unleavened bread for seven days and hold a solemn assembly to the LORD your God on the seventh day; you must not work on it.

You must not sacrifice to the Lord your God an ox or a sheep that has a blemish or any defect because this is an abomination to the Lord your God.

If a man or woman is found in your midst—within any of the gates that the Lord your God gives you—doing what is evil in the eyes of the Lord your God by transgressing his covenant, and has gone and served other gods and worshipped them, or the sun or moon or any of the host of heaven, which I have not commanded; and if this is reported to you and you have heard of it, then you shall do as the Lord your God has commanded. If that abomination truly has been done, then you shall bring out that man and stone him to death. The one who is to die shall be put to death based on the testimony of two or three witnesses; however, he shall not be put to death based on the testimony of one witness. The hands of the witnesses will be the first to put him to death, followed by the hands of the entire population. As a result, you must expel the evil from your midst.

The Levitical priests, and indeed the entire tribe of Levi, shall have no inheritance or portion with Israel but shall eat the Lord's fire offerings which are his portion.

And if a Levite moves from any of your towns in Israel, where he is living, to the place that the Lord chooses, he shall minister in the name of the Lord his God, as do all his countrymen, the Levites who stand before the Lord. Aside from the proceeds from the sale of his family estate, they will be served equal portions of food.

When you enter the land that the Lord has promised you, do not mimic the practices of those around you. No one shall be found among you who makes their child pass through the fire and practices divination, a sorcerer, one who casts spells, interprets, consults ghosts or spirits, or consults the dead.

The Lord then responded to me and said, "They are correct. I will raise up a prophet like you among them; I will place my words in his mouth, and he will speak only as I direct him. And he who does not practice is diligent in what he will say in my name. I will hold you accountable.

The Lord shall separate three cities for you, one in each of the land which He shall give you to possess as an inheritance, which you shall inherit as your forever homes. You shall prepare the way and divide the borders of your land, which the Lord your God shall cause you to inherit into three parts so that every manslayer may flee there.

And if the Lord your God enlarges your border, as he promised to your forefathers, and gives you all the land he promised to give to your forefathers if you keep this entire commandment by carrying it out, as I command you today, by loving the Lord your God and walking always in his ways—then you can add three cities to these three. Do this, that innocent blood may not be shed in the midst of your land, which Yahweh your God has given you for an inheritance, and that blood may not be on you.

In your inheritance that you will hold in the land that the Lord your God is giving to you to possess, you shall not remove your neighbor's boundary marker that previous generations have set.

A single witness shall not come forward against a person in connection with any iniquity or sin that he may have committed; a charge shall be sustained on the evidence of two or three witnesses. If a malicious witness comes forward to accuse someone of wrongdoing, both parties involved in the dispute must appear before the Lord, the priests, and the judges in office at the time. The judges must then conduct a thorough investigation. If the witness is found to be a false witness who has falsely testified against his brother, you must punish him as he had intended to punish his brother. As a result, you must expel the evil from your midst.

Then the rest will hear about it and be terrified, and they will never do such a thing in your presence again. Your eyes shall not be moved by pity: his life for his life, an eye for an eye, a tooth for a tooth, and a hand for a hand, a foot for a foot;

"You shall not be afraid when you go to war against your enemies and see horses and chariots and a people greater in number than you because the LORD your God, who brought you up from Egypt, is with you. And when you're about to go to battle, the priest will approach the people and say to them, "Hear, O Israel, you're about to go to war against your enemies today." Do not be discouraged, afraid, panicked, or terrified of them, for the LORD your God is with you, fighting for you against your foes and giving you victory."

The officers will then address the crowd, asking, "Has anyone built a new house that has not yet been dedicated?" Allow him to leave and return to his home, lest he perish in the battle and the shrine be dedicated to someone else. Is there anyone who has planted a vineyard but hasn't yet harvested the fruit? Allow him to leave and return to his home, lest he perish in the battle and the fruit be used by someone else. Is anyone out there engaged to a woman but hasn't yet married her?

Allow him to leave and return to his home, lest he be killed in battle, and someone else marries her." And the judges will address the people further, saying, "Is anyone afraid and fainthearted?" Allow him to leave and return to his home, lest his neighbor's heart melts as much as his own." When the officers have finished speaking with the people, they will appoint army commanders to lead them.

But the LORD your God would not hearken to Balaam, but the LORD, your God, would turn the curse into a blessing for you because the LORD your God loves you. You will not promote their welfare or prosperity as long as you live. You shall not despise the Edomite, for he is your countryman; you shall not despise the Egyptian, for you were a foreigner living in his land. If one of you becomes unclean because of the nocturnal emission, he's going outside the camp, and he's not allowed to enter the camp. But when evening comes, he shall bathe in water; when the sun sets, he may return to the camp.

You must also have a place outside the camp] where you can relieve yourself, and you must have a spade among your tools, which you must use to restore and cover your excrement when you sit outside. To save you and to punish your enemies, the LORD will walk among you to protect and to deliver.

You shall not return a slave to his master who has escaped from his master to you. He is free to live with you, in your midst, in any location he chooses in any of your towns, and you are not to oppress him. There shall be no cult prostitute among Israel's daughters nor Israel's sons. You shall not bring the wages of a prostitute [or the wages of a male prostitute] into the house of the LORD your God to pay any vow because both are abominations to the LORD your God. You are not permitted to charge interest to your countryman on money, food, or anything else that may accrue interest. You may charge interest to a foreigner, but not to a fellow citizen, so that the LORD your God may bless you in all you do in the land you are about to take possession of.

When you make a vow to the LORD your God, you must not delay in paying it, or the LORD your God will hold you accountable, and you will commit sin. However, you will have no sin if you do not vow. You must be careful to carry out what comes from your lips, just as you have sworn to the LORD your God as a freewill offering what you have promised with your mouth. You may eat your fill of grapes when you visit your neighbor's vineyard, but you must not put any in your basket. You may pluck the ears with your hands if you go into your neighbor's standing grain, but you must not use a sickle on his standing grain.

If a man takes a wife and marries her, but she does not find favor in his eyes because he finds something objectionable about her, he shall write her a bill of divorce, place it in her hand, and send her away from his home. She could then go on to marry another man. And if the latter husband divorces her and gives her away or consigns her to a far country, her former husband who sent her away will not have the right to get her back. Because that is an abomination in the eyes of the LORD, you must not bring sin into the land that the LORD your God is giving you as an inheritance.

When a man marries a new wife, he is not required to join the army or perform any duties for a year; instead, he is free to stay home and enjoy his new wife. No one shall pledge a mill or an upper millstone because he would be pledging a man's life. If a man is caught kidnapping one of his fellow Israelites and mistreating or selling him, he will be put to death. As a result, you must purge the evil from your midst.

Take care to observe and act following all that the Levitical priests teach you to avoid an outbreak of leprosy; just as I commanded them, you must take care. Keep in mind what the LORD your God did to Miriam on the way out of Egypt. You must not go into your neighbor's house to take his pledge when you make him a loan of any kind. You must stand outside and wait for the man you lend the money to, to bring the pledge to you.

And if he is a poor man, you must not sleep with his pledge in your possession; instead, you must return it to him when the sun sets so that he may sleep in his garment and bless you. And it will be considered a good deed by you in the eyes of the LORD your God.

You must not take advantage of a hired servant who is poor and in need, whether he is a citizen of your country or a foreigner who lives in your town. You must pay him his wages every day before the sun sets because he is poor and has his heart set on it. Otherwise, he may complain to the LORD about you, and you will be guilty of sin. If two people have a disagreement and go to court, the judges will decide between them, vindicating the righteous and convicting the guilty. If the guilty party deserves to be flogged, the judge will have him lie down and be beaten in front of him with the appropriate number of strokes. He may give him forty lashes, but no more, so that he does not beat him with many more stripes than these do, and you consider your neighbor to be degraded.

When the ox treads out the grain, you must not muzzle it. If two brothers live together and one dies without a son, the deceased's wife shall not be married to a stranger outside the family; her husband's brother shall go into her and take her for himself as a wife, performing the duties of a husband's brother to her. And the firstborn son or daughter she bears will take his deceased brother's name so that his name will not be blotted out of Israel.

If the man does not want to marry his brother's wife, his brother's wife must go up to the elders at the gate and say, "My husband's brother refuses to raise up a name in Israel for his brother; he will not perform the duty of a husband's brother to me." The elders of his city will summon him and speak with him; and if he persists in saying, "I do not want to take her," [his brother's wife] will come to him in front of the elders and pull his shoe from his foot and spit in his face, declaring, "This is what happens to the man who does not build up his brother's house." His line will be known throughout Israel as "The House of Him Whose Sandal Was Pulled Off."

You may not have two types of weights in your bag, large and small. You may not have two types of measures in your home: large and small. You shall have only an accurate and honest weight, only an accurate and honest measure, so that your days in the land that the LORD your God is giving you may be prolonged. All who act dishonestly and do such things are an abomination to the LORD your God.

And when you enter the land which your God gives you for an inheritance, and harvest its first fruits, you must take them and bring them to the temple of the LORD your God so that he may reside there. "I profess this day before the LORD your God [that I have come to the land which the LORD swore to our ancestors to give us," you shall say to the priest who is officiating at the time. The priest will then take the basket from your hands and place it before the LORD your God's altar. And you shall respond and say to the LORD your God, "My father was a wandering Aramean who went down into Egypt and settled there with a small number of people." And there, he grew into a great, powerful, and populous nation.

While in mourning, I did not eat from it, remove any of it while unclean, or offer any of it to the dead. I have obeyed all that you have commanded me because I have heard the voice of the LORD my God. Look down from your holy throne, from heaven, and bless your people Israel and the land you promised to our forefathers, a land flowing with milk and honey.

The people were then commanded by Moses and the elders of Israel to "keep all these commandments which I command you this day." And when you cross the Jordan into the land that the LORD your God is giving you, you must erect large stones for yourself and plaster them. Then, when you have crossed over, you shall write on them all the words of this law, so that] you may enter the land that the LORD your God is giving you—a land flowing with milk and honey—just as the LORD, the God of your ancestors, has promised you.

And after you have crossed the Jordan, you shall set up these stones in Mount Ebal, which I command you today, and coat them with plaster. And there you shall construct an altar to the LORD your God out of stones, on which no iron tool shall be used. You must build the altar of the LORD your God out of unhewn stones and offer burnt offerings to the LORD your God on it. You will offer peace offerings and eat there, and you will rejoice in the presence of the LORD your God. Then you must write all of the words of this law very clearly on the stones.

The Levitical priests and Moses then addressed all the people of Israel, saying, "Be silent, O Israel, and listen!" You have now become the LORD your God's people. As a result, you must obey the LORD your God's voice and keep his commandments and statutes, which I am commanding you today."

The one who kills his neighbor in secret is cursed. And everyone will say, "Amen." Whoever takes a bribe to kill an innocent person will be cursed. And all the people shall say, "Amen." Whoever does not carry out the words of this law will be cursed. And everyone in the room will say, "Amen." And Moses had finished speaking all of these words to the entire nation of Israel. "I am a hundred and twenty years old today; I can no longer go out and come in, and the LORD has said to me, 'You shall not cross over the Jordan,'" he said to them. The LORD, your God, will cross over ahead of you; he will destroy these nations before you, and you will possess them; and Joshua, as the LORD has spoken, will cross over ahead of you. And the LORD will do to them what he did to the Amorites' kings Sihon and Og, as well as their land when he destroyed them.

And the LORD will deliver them to you, and you must treat them according to every commandment that I have given you. Be strong and courageous, and do not fear or be terrified because of them; for the LORD your God is with you; he will not fail you or forsake you."

"Be strong and courageous, for you shall go with this people into the land which the LORD has sworn to their forefathers to give them, and you shall cause them to inherit it," Moses said to Joshua in front of all Israel. And the LORD is the one who goes ahead of you; he will be with you, he will not let you down, he will not abandon you; do not be afraid or discouraged."

Then Moses wrote this law down in a book and gave it to the priests, the Levite sons who carried the LORD's Ark of the Covenant, and to all the elders of Israel. "You shall read this law before all Israel in their hearing at the end of every seven years, in the] set time of the year of remission, during the feast of tabernacles, when all Israel comes to appear before the LORD your God in the place which he shall choose," Moses commanded. Assemble the people, men, women, and children, as well as your foreigner who is within your gates, so that they may hear, learn, and fear the LORD their God, and be careful to carry out all the words of this law; and so that their children, who have never heard it, may hear and learn to fear the LORD their God as long as you live in the land to which you are crossing the Jordan.

"Behold, your days are approaching when you must die; call Joshua, and present yourselves in the tent of meeting so that I may commission him," the LORD said to Moses. So Moses and Joshua went to the tent of meeting and presented themselves.

Then, in the form of a pillar of cloud, the LORD appeared in the tent, and the pillar of cloud stood at the tent's door. "Behold, you shall sleep with your ancestors; and this people will rise up and prostitute themselves to the strange gods of the land, where they go to be among them, and will forsake me and break the covenant that I have made with them," the LORD said to Moses.

Then in that day, I will abandon you and hide my face from them, and they will be devoured, and many evils and troubles will come upon them, so that they will say in that day, "Have not these disasters come upon us because the Lord my God is not among us?" And I'll surely hide my face from them on that day because of all their evil by turning to other gods.

And this is the blessing with which Moses, the man of God, blessed the Israelites before he died. The LORD descended from Sinai and ascended from Seir upon them; he shone forth from Mount Paran and descended from the ten thousands of holy ones, and a fiery law was given to them at his right hand. Indeed, he loves his people; all of his holy ones are in your hands; they marched at your feet, and he gave orders to everyone. Moses gave us a law and an inheritance for Jacob's assembly. And he reigned as king in Jeshurun, when the people's leaders gathered, all the tribes of Israel in one place.

Allow Reuben to live, not perish, and don't limit his numbers. And this is Judah's blessing: he said, "Listen, O LORD, to Judah's voice, and bring him into his people." "Your Thummim and your Urim are with your godly one, whom you proved at Massah, with whom you contended at the waters of Meribah; who said of his father and mother, 'I have not seen him;' neither did he recognize his brothers or acknowledge his children," he said of Levi. They have kept your covenant and observed your word. They will teach Jacob and Israel your laws and ordinances. They will place incense in front of you and a complete burnt offering on your altar. Bless his substance, O LORD, and accept his handwork; crush the loins of those who rise up against him and those who hate him, so that they do not rise again."

"The LORD's beloved shall dwell in safety by him," he said of Benjamin. He wraps himself around him all day and lives between his shoulders."

"Blessed by the LORD be his land, for the precious things of heaven, for the dew, and for the deep that lies beneath, and for the precious things of the sun's fruits, and for the precious things of the months' growth, and for the finest products of the ancient mountains, and for the precious things of the everlasting hills, and for the precious things of the earth," he said of Joseph.

Let the blessing descend on Joseph's head, as well as on the crown of his head who was separated from his brothers. His herd's firstborn—majesty is his! His horns resemble those of a wild ox. He will push the people, all of them, to the ends of the earth with him. And they are Ephraim's ten thousand and Manasseh's thousands."

"Rejoice, Zebulun, in your going out, and, Issachar, in your tents," he said to Zebulun. They will summon the people to their mountain, where they will offer righteous sacrifices. They will gorge themselves on the bounty of the seas and the buried treasures of the sand. "Blessed is he who enlarges Gad; he lives like a lion and tears the arm and the crown of the head," he said of Gad. He chose the best part for himself because a commander's portion was reserved; when he arrived at the heads of the people, he carried out the LORD's righteousness and his ordinances with Israel." "Dan is a lion whelp who leaps out of Bashan," he said of Dan. He also said of Naphtali, "O Naphtali, satisfied with favor and full of the LORD's blessing, possess the west and the south." "Blessed be Asher with children; let him be acceptable to his brothers, and let him dip his foot in oil," he said of Asher.

Happy are you, O Israel; who can compare to you, a people saved by the LORD, the shield of your protection and the sword of your victory? Your adversaries will submit to you, and you will walk on their high ground. And Moses ascended Mount Nebo, to the top of Pisgah, which is opposite Jericho, from the plains of Moab. And the LORD showed him all of the lands, from Gilead to Dan, and all of Naphtali, and all of Ephraim and Manasseh, and all of Judah, to the western sea, and the Negev, and the plain of Jericho, the city of palm trees, to Zoar.

"This is the land that I swore to Abraham, Isaac, and Jacob, saying, 'I will give it to your descendants; I have allowed you to see it with your eyes, but you shall not cross over there," the LORD said to him.

According to the LORD's word, Moses, the LORD's servant, died there in the land of Moab. They buried him in a valley in Moab's land, opposite Beth-Peor, but no one knows where he was buried to this day. When Moses died, he was a hundred and twenty years old, but his sight and strength had not deteriorated. The Israelites wept for Moses for thirty days on the plains of Moab, and then the days of mourning for Moses ended.

JUBILEE

The Book of Jubilee is a fascinating ancient Jewish work that most modern readers are unfamiliar with. Jubilee contains an account of things revealed to Moses during his forty days on Mount Sinai (Exod 24:18) and was revealed to him by an angel. It provides an overview of the history of humanity and God's chosen people until Moses' time.

This book, which is usually categorized as a "rewritten Bible," may be divided into seven sections:

- An Introduction (chap. 1), in which God describes the apostasy of his people and their future restoration.
- A Primeval History (chaps. 2–4), dealing with the creation and Adam.
- Noah's lives and journey (chaps. 5–10).
- Stories about Abraham (chaps. 11–23:8).
- Abraham's death (chaps. 23:9–32).
- Jacob and his family (chaps. 24–45).
- Stories about Moses (chaps. 46–50).

Jubilees was part of the most ancient canon of the Ethiopic church before the discovery of the Dead Sea Scrolls and was known to scholars in Greek, Syriac, Latin, and Ethiopic translations. Many people were surprised and intrigued by the discovery of a large number of Jubilee manuscripts at Qumran.

Joshua

Only two scrolls of Joshua's book were discovered in the Judean Desert. Still, one has a significant impact, and several previously unknown parabiblical works related to Joshua discovered among the scrolls have added to our understanding of the ancient world. According to the traditional story, Joshua leads the people across the Jordan, battles for Jericho defeats the city of Ai, and then travels twenty miles north to Shechem to build an altar on Mount Ebal, opposite Mount Gerizim, where the Samaritans would later center their religion. He then marches south, abandoning the newly constructed altar and leaving it vulnerable in enemy territory.

This means Joshua would have built the first altar in the Promised Land right after crossing the Jordan and before starting any conquest battles. Of course, Joshua would have immediately erected an altar at Gilgal in thanksgiving to fulfill the land's promise and sanctify the land to the Lord. Gilgal remained a significant place of worship, whereas Mount Ebal was never mentioned again as a place of worship for Israel.

"Select one from each tribe and give them this command: Pick up twelve stones from the middle of the Jordan, carry them over with you, and set them down in the place where you camp tonight," the Lord said to Joshua after the entire nation had crossed the Jordan. After that, he read all of the words of the law, blessings, and curses precisely as they were written in the law book. There was not a single commandment that Moses gave Joshua that Joshua did not read in front of the entire people of Israel, including the women and children and the strangers who lived among them.

"Make for yourselves flint knives, and circumcise the children of Israel again," the Lord said to Joshua at that time. So Joshua made himself flint knives and circumcised the Israelites at the Hill of the Foreskins. And this is why Joshua had them circumcised: after leaving Egypt, all of the people who had come out of Egypt, all of the males of military age, had died in the desert along the way.

For everyone who had come out had been circumcised, but those who were born in the desert on the way out of Egypt had not been circumcised. Because they did not obey the Lord—those to whom the Lord swore that they would not see the land that the Lord had sworn to their ancestors that he would give us, a land flowing with milk and honey—the Israelites journeyed forty years in the desert until the entire nation, that is, the men of military age who had come out of Egypt, died because they did not obey the Lord. So Joshua circumcised their sons, whom he raised in their place; they had been uncircumcised because they had not been circumcised along the way. The crowd erupts in applause when the ram's horn blows a long blast, and the trumpet blows. The city wall will then crumble, and the people will charge forward, each one straight ahead. "Take up the ark of the covenant, and have seven priests carry seven rams' horns ahead of the ark of the Lord," Joshua, son of Nun, told the [priests]. "Go forward, march around the city, and let the armed guard march ahead of the ark of the Lord," Joshua told the people. Following Joshua's speech to the people, the seven priests carrying the seven rams' horns marched before the Lord, blowing their trumpets, and the ark of the Lord's covenant followed them. The armed guard advanced ahead of the priests blowing the trumpets, and the rear guard pursued the ark while the priests blew the trumpets. Joshua issued the following command to the people: "Do not shout, do not let your voices be heard, do not let a word come out of your mouth until I tell you, Shout! Then you will yell".

As a result, the Israelites cannot stand in front of their enemies; instead, they turn their backs on them, not their faces, as they have been condemned to destruction. I won't be with you any longer unless you destroy everything you have that has been dedicated to destruction. Rise and sanctify the people, saying, "Sanctify yourselves" for tomorrow. The Lord, the God of Israel, says to Israel, "There is a devoted thing in your midst." You won't be able to stand up to your foes until you get rid of the devoted thing from your midst, by tribes, [you shall come forward] in the morning. Households will then bring forward the Lord's chosen tribe. The Lord's selected household will then come forward individually. Then the chosen one among them will be consumed by fire and everything he owns because he broke the Lord's covenant and brought shame upon Israel."

Then Adonizedek, the king of Jerusalem, sent a message to Hoham, the king of Hebron, Piram, the king of Jarmuth, Japhia, the king of Lachish, and Debir, the king of Eglon, saying, "Come up to me and help me defeat Gibeon because it has made peace with Joshua and Israel." So the five kings of the Amorites—the kings of Jerusalem, Hebron, Jarmuth, Lachish, and Eglon—joined forces and marched on Gibeon, encamped there, and waged war against it.

"Do not be afraid of them, for I have given them to you," the Lord told Joshua. They won't be able to stand a chance against you." Joshua appeared out of nowhere, having marched from Gilgal all night. The Lord put them in a panic in front of Israel, who crushed them at Gibeon and pursued them to Bethhoron, attacking them all the way to Azekah and Makkedah. Then, as they fled Israel and descended from Bethhoron, the Lord rained down stones from the sky on them all the way to Azekah, killing them. The hailstones killed more of them than the Israelites killed with the sword.

This was Manasseh's fate because he was Joseph's firstborn son. Machir, Manasseh's firstborn and father of Gilead, was given Gilead and Bashan because he was a warrior. After that, portions were assigned to the rest of

Manasseh's descendants based on their clans: Abiezer, Helek, Asriel, Shechem, Hepher, and Shemida.

By their clans, these were the male children of Manasseh, Joseph's son. Only daughters were born to Zelophehad, son of Hepher, son of Gilead, son of Machir, son of Manasseh. Mahlah and Noah, Hoglah, Milcah, and Tirzah are the names of his daughters. "The Lord commanded Moses to give us an inheritance among our brothers," they said as they presented themselves to Eleazar, the priest, Joshua, son of Nun, and the leaders. As a result, he gave them an inheritance among their father's brothers, according to the Lord's word.

Manasseh had three heights within Issachar and Asher: Bethshean and its towns, the people of Endor and its towns, Ibleam and its towns, the people of Dor and its towns, the people of Taanach and its towns, and the people of Megiddo and its towns. The Manassites, on the other hand, we're unable to drive out the inhabitants of those cities, and the Canaanites were adamant about remaining in the area. The Israelites later subjected the Canaanites to forced labor as they grew stronger, but they did not completely expel them. "Why have you given us an inheritance of only one lot and one district?" the Josephites asked Joshua. "If you are a numerous people, go up to the forest and clear land for yourselves there in the land of the Perizzites and Rephaim, insofar as the hill country of Ephraim is too small for you," Joshua replied.

JUDGES

Gideon and his fleece, Jephthah's unfortunate daughter, and Samson and Delilah are just a few of the well-known characters from the book of Judges. On the other hand, the Qumran community seemed to be more interested in the weightier matters of law and the poetic praise of the Psalms than in the "historical books" narratives. Joshua's sparse pattern (only two scrolls) continues in Chronicles (only one scroll!).

Chapter 1

Ezra lived on a great deal of money. Israel retreated from Midian and erected strongholds in secret as a result. The Amalekites or Midianites may emerge from the desert whenever Israel plants its fields. They camped against the soil all the way to Gaza. No animals survived, including sheep, oxen, or donkeys. They indeed brought their livestock and camels; an endless number of them came in. They planned to destroy the country. As a result of Midian, the Israelites, they cried out to the Lord. Then an angel of the Lord appeared while Joash the Abiezrite's son was crushing grapes under an oak to conceal it. "The Lord will be with you," the Lord's messenger appeared and said Sir, if God is on our side, then what happened to us?" Gideon inquired," Once upon a time, our ancestors said to us, "Didn't the Lord free us from Egypt?" Now the Lord has given us over to the hands of Midian.

"Take the meat and the unleavened cakes, lay them on this rock, and pour out the broth," God's messenger said. And he went ahead and did it. Then the Lord's messenger touched the meat and unleavened cakes with the tip of his staff, and flames rose from the rock and consumed the meat and unleavened cakes. The Lord's messenger then vanished from his view. When Gideon realized he was the Lord's messenger, he exclaimed, "Oh no, Lord God!" I have seen the Lord's messenger face to face."

"Please ask in the hearing of all the people of Shechem: 'What is better for you that all seventy sons of Jerubbaal rule over you or that one rule over you?" Abimelech, son of Jerubbaal, went to Shechem, to his mother's brothers, and spoke with them and the entire clan of his maternal grandfather's family. Keep in mind that I'm your flesh and blood.' As a result, his mother's brothers spoke these things about him in front of the entire town of Shechem. "He is our kinsman," they reasoned, so they were inclined to follow Abimelech. So they gave him seventy silver pieces from Baal-temple, berith's which Abimelech used to hire] worthless and reckless men to follow him. Then he went to his father's house in Ophrah and stoned his brothers, Jerubbaal's sons, a total of seventy people to death. However, Jotham, Jerubbaal's youngest son, was spared because he hid himself. Then everyone from Shechem, as well as everyone from Beth Millo, gathered and went to Shechem to make Abimelech king by the oak of the pillar.

Who was Abimeleus? God's Son (Joseph) said Jerba's son and office Zebul served the men of Hamor, didn't he? Why should we obey him? "I am only sorry that this group isn't under my control." "Be out and fight," they said to Abimelech. The Lord of Zebul was incensed to hear what Gaal, son of Ebed, speak. They are sending messengers to warn Abimelech and his kin, and they are arriving at Shechem. Abimelech pursued them all the way to the city gate, and many of them died on the way. Abimelech fled from Shechem while Zebul stayed behind.

The people went out into the fields the next day, and someone informed Abimelech. So he divided his army into three companies and set up an ambush in the fields. He kept an eye on the people, and when they left the city, he rose up against them and attacked them. So each of the troops cut a branch and piled it against the stronghold, following Abimelech's lead setting the stronghold on fire over those inside. As a result, all of the people in Shechem's tower, about a thousand men and women, died.

Then they said, "Listen, every year in Shiloh, north of Bethel, east of the highway that goes up from Bethel to Shechem, and south of Lebonah, there is a Lord's feast." "Go and lie in wait in the vineyards and watch to see if the women of Shiloh come out to participate in the dances," they told the Benjaminites. Then come out of the vineyards, each of you taking a wife from the Shiloh women, and go to Benjamin's land. 'Be generous with us about them because none of us took a wife in battle,' we will tell their fathers or brothers when they come to complain to us. And you are innocent because you did not give them to them.'

The Benjaminites did this. The dancing women's wives were forcibly carried away in large numbers. Then they returned to their inheritance, rebuilding and living in the cities they had inherited. As a result, the Israelites dispersed at that time, each to his tribe and family. All of them returned to their inheritance. There was no king in Israel at the time. Everyone did what they thought was right in their own eyes.

"Lord of hosts, if you truly look upon the misery of your servant and remember me, and do not forget your servant but give your servant a son, then I will give him, and no razor shall cross his head," Hannah said as she continued to pray before the Lord. Her lips moved, but her voice was not heard. She was speaking [in her heart. As a result, Eli assumed she was inebriated.

"My heart rejoices in God," Hannah prayed, "and my strength is exalted in the Lord." My mouth speaks boldly against my enemies because I rejoice in your salvation. The Lord is the only one who is truly holy. Our God is the only one who is completely righteous. You're the only one who can claim to be holy. Our God is unlike any other rock you've ever seen. Stop being so arrogant in your speech. Allow no arrogance to slip out of your mouth. Because the Lord is a God of knowledge, he judges his actions.

The bows of the mighty men are shattered, but those who fall gain strength. Those who are well fed hire themselves out for bread, while those who were hungry are no longer hungry. The barren woman bears seven children, but the large-family woman languishes. The Lord kills and then raises the dead. He goes to Sheol and then returns. The Lord creates both rich and poor people. He debases and exalts at the same time. He raises the poor from the ashes and the needy from the dust. He elevates them to the status of princes and bestows upon them an honorary seat. The Lord owns the earth's pillars and built the world on top of them. He guards the path of his faithful, but the wicked are silenced in the darkness.

Samuel served as a minister. The boy wore an ephod every year when his parents went up to the temple to offer the annual sacrifice. The LORD restored [this poor mother with a] woman instead of the ones Eli had prayed for and dedicated to him. Hannah gave birth to three children, one son, and two daughters.

Meanwhile, the boy had faith. Eli, a 98-year-year-old at the time, heard of his son's misdeeds.

As a result, he asked them, "Why do you do these things?" All the Lord's people have told me about your evil deeds. No, my sons, the news I've received isn't good. Do not behave in this manner. The report that I've heard God's people passing around isn't good. If one person commits a grave sin against another, he will seek forgiveness from the Lord. But who will intercede for someone who sins against the Lord?" However, they did not heed the advice because it was God's will to put them to death. Samuel, on the other hand, grew in stature and favor with the Lord and the people.

"Thus says the Lord, I did indeed reveal myself to your father's house when they were slaves of Pharaoh's house in Egypt," a man of God said to Eli. Out of all the tribes of Israel, I chose your father's house to be my priest, to go up to my altar to burn incense and wear the ephod. I gave all of the children of Israel's fire offerings to your father's house.

Why do you look down on my sacrifice and offering, which I commanded for my habitation, and honor your sons over me, fattening yourself on the best of all Israel's offerings in my presence?

As a result, the Lord says, "I declare, your house and your father will be among you always." The very Lord forbids it. I curse those who do not respect me." the time is coming when I cut off your and your father's strength; I will deal only with his eyes and cause misery if you don't get rid of any of mine. Humanity will exterminate all of your progeny. Thus, the death of your two sons, Hophni and Phineas, will be a sign for you.

The youngster Under Eli's leadership, Samuel served the Lord. In those days, the Lord's word was uncommon. Visions were few and far between. Eli, who had weak eyes and couldn't see, was sleeping in his place at the time. When Samuel was sleeping in the Lord's temple before the lamp of God went out, the Lord called out, "Samuel." "Here I am," he replied. As a result, Samuel told him everything and kept nothing hidden from him. "He is the Lord," he added. "Allow him to do what he thinks is right."

The Lord was with Samuel as he grew, and none of his words fell to the ground. Samuel's status as a prophet of the Lord was confirmed throughout Israel, from Dan to Beersheba.

So they summoned all of the Philistine lords and asked, "What shall we do with the ark [of the God of Israel?" "Let them bring the ark of the God of Israel around to Gath," they replied. As a result, they brought the ark of God to Gath. Then, when they brought it to Gath, the Lord's hand came down on the city, causing it to flee in terror. He infected the city's citizens, both small and large, with a tumor outbreak. As a result, the ark of the God of Israel was sent to Ekron.

The Ekronites then cried out, "Why have you brought around the ark of the God of Israel to kill us and our people?" when the ark of God arrived in Ekron. "Send away the ark of the God of Israel, and let it return to its place so that it does not kill us and our people," they sent for and gathered all the lords of the Philistines. Because there was fear of the Lord all over the city. God's hand was weighty there. The people who did not die were afflicted with tumors, and the city's cries reached the Heavens.

The ark of the Lord spent seven months in Philistine territory. The Philistines summoned the priests, diviners, and magicians, asking, "What should we do with the Lord's ark?" "Tell us how to return it to its proper location." They replied, "Do not return the ark of the covenant of the Lord, God of Israel, empty." You must make a sin offering to him. Then you will be healed and make reparation for your sins. "Will he keep his hand on us? "

They asked, "What is the sin offering we are to return to him?" They replied, "Five golden tumors, according to the number of Philistine lords." "Because you all, as well as your lords, were afflicted by a single plague. As a result, make images of tumors and mice destroying the land, and you'll give Israel's God glory. Maybe he'll let you, your gods, and your land out of his clutches.

Why would you, like the Egyptians and Pharaoh, harden your hearts?

Was it only after he humiliated them that they released the people and went their separate ways? Get a new cart and two milk cows who have never been yoked. Cows should be grazed and tied to the cart. Separate them from their calves, however, and bring them home."

The cows were heading straight for Beth-shemesh. They followed the highway, lowing as they went and making no turns to the right or left, while the Philistine lords pursued them all the way to the Beth-shemesh border. The people of Beth-shemesh were reaping their wheat harvest in the valley when they looked up and saw the ark, which filled them with joy.

The five Philistine lords saw this and returned to Ekron the next day. The Philistines returned these golden tumors to the Lord as a sin offering: one for Ashdod, one for Gaza, one for Ashkelon, one for Gath, and one for Ekron. All the Philistine cities belonging to the five lords' fortified cities [and their country villages] were numbered according to the golden mice. The large stone on which the ark of the Lord was placed remains a witness to this day in Joshua's Beth-shemeshite field. "Who is able to stand in the presence of this holy Lord?" the people of Beth-shemesh wondered. "From here, where should the ark go?" "The Philistines have brought back the ark of the Lord," they sent messengers to the people of Kiriath-jearim. Come down here and take it with you."

Now pay attention to them. Only a strong warning and instruction in the customs of the king who will rule over them will suffice. So Samuel told the people who had asked him for a king everything the Lord had said to him. "These are the customs of the king who will rule over you: He will take your sons and use them for his benefit, some to serve with his chariots, some to be his horsemen, and some to run in front of his chariots," he said. "Others will be captains of thousands and fifties; he will appoint.

He'll appoint some to plow [his] land and reap his harvest, while other will work on his war weapons and chariot equipment. He'll also take you daughters and train them to be perfumers, cooks, and bakers. He'll tak the best of your fields, vineyards, and olive groves and give them to hi entourage. He'll take a tenth of your seed and the harvest from you vineyard and give it to his officers and servants. He'll use you manservants and maidservants, as well as the best of your young men and donkeys, for his own purposes. He'll rob you of a tenth of your flocks You'll be his servants as well. When that day arrives, you will cry out fo help because of your king, whom you chose for yourself, but the Lord will not answer you in those days." However, the people refused to listen to Samuel's advice. "No," they replied. "We must be ruled by a king.

Then, like all the other nations, we will have a judge, a leader, and a king to lead us and fight our battles." "Look, there is a man of God in thi city," the servant informed Saul. Everything he says is certain to happer because he is so respected. Now, let's get started. Perhaps he'll point us ir the right direction." "But if we go, what shall we bring the man?" Sau continued. Because the bread in our sacks has run out, and we have nothing to offer the man of God. "What exactly do we have?" They me young women going out to draw water as they walked up the road to the city and asked, "Is the seer here?" "He is," they responded. "Look at how far ahead of you he is. Please hurry. He'd just arrived in town because the people are making a sacrifice at the highest point today."

I'll send you a man from Benjamin's land around this time tomorrow. You will anoint him prince over my people Israel, and he will deliver them from the Philistines' grasp. Because their cries have reached me, I have looked on my people. The Lord said to Samuel when he saw Saul, "This is the man I spoke to you about." This man will be in charge of my people "Please tell me where the seer's house is," Saul said as he approached Samuel inside the city. "I am he," Samuel replied to Saul. "Continue ahead of me to the highest point because you'll be eating with me today. I'll send you off in the morning and inform you of everything that's on your mind.

Do not be concerned about the donkeys that you lost three days ago; they have been found. And for whom is everything in Israel desirable? Isn't it for you and your entire family at your father's house?" "Am I not a Benjamite, the smallest of Israel's tribes?" Saul replied. "Isn't my family the least of all the families in Benjamin's tribe? So, why are you speaking to me in this manner?" But Samuel led Saul and his servant into the hall and seated them at the head of the thirty people who had been invited. "Bring the portion I gave you, the one I told you to set aside," Samuel said to the cook. So the cook placed the leg, and whatever was on it in front of Saul.

Nahash, the Ammonite king, brutally oppressed the Gadites and Reubenites. All of their right eyes were removed, and Israel was filled with fear and trembling. Except for seven thousand men who escaped the Ammonites and went to Jabesh-Gilead, none of the Israelites in the region beyond the Jordan had their right eye put out by Nahash, king of the Ammonites.

Nahash the Ammonite then went up and besieged Jabesh-Gilead after about a month. "Make a covenant with us, and we will serve you," all the people of Jabesh said to Nahash. "I will make it with you on this condition: that I gouge out the right eye of every one of you and thus disgrace all Israel," Nahash the Ammonite said to them. "Whoever does not march out behind Saul and Samuel, so shall it be done to his oxen," he said, cutting a yoke of oxen in pieces and sending them throughout Israel by messengers. The people were terrified of the Lord and came out as one man.

Saul divided the people into three companies the next day, and they invaded the camp and slaughtered the Ammonites during the morning watch until the heat of the day set in. Those who made it were dispersed and no two of them were found together. The people asked Samuel, "Who said, 'Shall Saul reign over us?' Bring the men so we can put them to death." "Now, stand there so I can debate you in front of the Lord about all of the Lord's righteous acts for you and your forefathers.

When your forefathers cried out to the Lord while Jacob was in Egypt, the Lord sent Moses and Aaron to bring your forefathers out of Egypt and settle them here.

"Very well, if you revere and serve the Lord, listen to his voice, and do not rebel against the Lord's commandments, if you and the king who reigns over you both follow the Lord your God. But if you refuse to listen to the Lord's voice and rebel against His commandments, the Lord's hand will be against you, just as it was against your forefathers. Now, stand there and witness this great thing that the Lord is about to do right in front of your eyes. Isn't today wheat harvest? I'll ask the Lord to send thunder and rain, and you'll realize how wicked you've been in the eyes of the Lord by asking for a king for yourselves". As a result of Samuel's prayer, the Lord sent thunder and rain that day. The people were terrified of the Lord and Samuel after that. "Pray for your servants to the Lord your God so that we do not die," the people said to Samuel, "because we have added to our sins this evil of asking for a king for ourselves." The Israelites were in a bad mood that day because Saul had sworn an oath to the army, saying, "Cursed be anyone who eats any food until evening, and I have avenged myself on my enemies."

As a result, no one tried the food. The entire army marched into the woods, where there was honey on the ground. The honey dripped down when the army entered the forest, but no one put his hand to his mouth because the troops feared the oath. On the other hand, Jonathan had not been aware that his father had taken the army under oath.

His eyes lit up as he stretched out the staff in his hand, dipped the end in the honeycomb, and put his hand to his mouth. "Your father strictly charged the army with an oath, 'Cursed be anyone who [eats food today,'" one of the people said. As a result, the troops were ineffective.

"And he has some connection to that famous fool!" It filled my mouth with flames." It would have been if the troops were allowed to gorge on the enemy's spoils. However, the number of Philistines who were killed that day was moderate. On the other hand, the troops set their sights on the plunder. They slaughtered sheep, oxen, and calves and drank their blood with no objection Look, the troops are committing a great sin by using the blood. He pronounced you untrustworthy Summon all the tribes, tell them to bring their oxen and sheep to me and slaughter them here. They brought their ox with them and slaughtered their cattle that night.

Now that Saul had taken control of Israel, he waged war against all of Israel's enemies, including Moab, the Ammonites, Edom, the king of Zobah, and the Philistines. He punished them everywhere he went. He fought valiantly, defeating the Amalekites and freeing Israel from the clutches of their oppressors. Jonathan, Ishvi, and Malchishua were now Saul's sons, and Merab, the firstborn, and Michal, the younger, were his two daughters. Ahinoam, the daughter of Ahimaaz, was Saul's wife. Abner, son of Ner, Saul's uncle, was the army's captain. Abiel had two sons: Kish, Saul's father, and Ner, Abner's father.

"Now, please forgive my transgression and join me in worshipping the Lord." "I will not return with you," Samuel replied to Saul. "The Lord has rejected you as king over Israel because you have rejected the Lord's word." Saul grabbed the hem of his robe and tore it as Samuel turned to leave. "Today, the Lord has torn the kingdom of Israel from you and given it to one of your neighbors, someone better than you," Samuel told him. "Furthermore, the Glory of Israel does not change his mind or repent because he is not a human being." "I have sinned," he replied. "But I beg you to honor me now, in front of my people's elders, and bring Israel back with you, so that I can worship the Lord your God."

As a result, Samuel returned with Saul to worship the Lord. "Bring Agag, king of the Amalekites, here to me," Samuel said. And Agag came to him cheerfully, believing that the threat of death had passed him by.

"How long will you mourn over Saul, knowing that I have rejected him as king over Israel?" the Lord asked Samuel. "Fill your horn with oil and get ready to go. I'm sending you to Jesse the Bethlehemite because I've chosen one of his sons to be my king." "How can I go?" Samuel asked. "Saul will kill me if he hears." "Take a heifer with you and say, 'I have come to sacrifice to the Lord,'" the Lord replied. "I'll show you what to do after you invite Jesse to the sacrifice. You are to anoint the one I show you for me."

As a result, Samuel followed the Lord's instructions. When he arrived in Bethlehem, the city elders greeted him with trembling and asked, "Seer, do you come in peace?" "Yes, in peace," he replied. "I've come to make an offering to the Lord. Come with me to the sacrifice and consecrate yourselves." Jesse and his sons were also consecrated and invited to the sacrifice.

He saw Eliab when they entered and thought to himself, "Surely the Lord's anointed is in his presence." "Do not regard his appearance or his tall frame because I have rejected him," the Lord told Samuel. "Because the Lord sees things differently than we do. Humans see what is on the outside, but the Lord sees what is on the inside."

Jesse then summoned Abinadab and requested that he present himself to Samuel. "The Lord has not chosen this one either," he added. Jesse then asked Shammah to come forward.

"The Lord has not chosen this one either," he added. Seven of Jesse's sons presented themselves to Samuel. "The Lord has not chosen these," Samuel told Jesse. "Are all your sons here?" Samuel asked Jesse. "There is still the youngest," he replied, "but he is tending the sheep." "Send for him," Samuel said to Jesse. "We're not going to sit down until he arrives."

The Philistines were on one side of a mountain, and Israel was on the other side of a mountain, with a valley between them. Then a champion from Gath named Goliath emerged from the Philistine camp.

He stood four cubits and a span tall. He wore a bronze helmet on his head and scale armor made of bronze that weighed 5,000 shekels. His legs were clad in bronze greaves, and a bronze javelin was slung between his shoulders. "Here is my elder daughter Merab," Saul said to David. "As a wife, I will give her to you. Simply fight the Lord's battles as a brave warrior on my behalf." "I will not touch him," Saul was thinking. "Instead, let the Philistines' might work against him." "Who am I, and what is my life or my father's family in Israel that I should be the king's son-in-law?" David asked Saul.

Saul attempted to impale him, but David escaped his grasp as he was pierced with the lance. David was able to escape that night. Saul sent messengers to check on David's house in the morning Either you save yourself, or you're a goner, Michal said. And so, David was let down from the window, and he escaped.

She covered it with goat's hair and placed it on the bed. as the king said, "He is feverish," Then Saul sent couriers to David to say, "Bring him to me, and I'll have him killed." When the messengers arrived, the idol had braided hair on its head. Why are you treating me like an enemy so you can get rid of him? Saul asked Michal. He told me, 'No.'" Do you think I should kill you?

When David learned that Saul was plotting against him, he told the priest Abiathar, "Bring the ephod here." "O Lord, God of Israel, your servant has undoubtedly heard that Saul intends to come to Keilah to destroy the city on my account," David said. "Will the citizens of Keilah hand me over to him? Will Saul, as your servant has heard, come down? Tell your servant, O Lord, God of Israel." "He will come down," the Lord said. "Will the men of Keilah surrender my men and me into the hands of Saul?" David asked. "They will," the Lord said. Then David and his men, who numbered around 600, arose and left Keilah, going wherever they could. When Saul learned that David had escaped from Keilah, he decided not to pursue him.

David stayed in the Ziph wilderness in the hill country and lived in the strongholds in the wilderness. Every day, Saul searched for him, but the Lord did not deliver him into his hands. While David was in the Ziph wilderness at Horesh, he noticed that Saul had come out to seek his life. Saul's son Jonathan got up and went to David at Horesh, encouraging him in the Lord. "Do not be afraid," he told him. "My father will not find you, David. You will be the king of Israel, and I will be your deputy. My father Saul, is also aware of this."

Nabal was the man's name, and Abigail was his wife's name. The woman was intelligent and attractive, but the man was obstinate and combative in the workplace. Nabal was the man's name. When David learned that Nabal was shearing his sheep in the desert, he dispatched ten servants. "Go up to Carmel, visit Nabal," David told the servants. "Greeting him in my name and wishing him a long life! Peace to you, your home, and everything you own. I just found out that you're shearing. Your shepherds were with us recently, and we did not mistreat them, and] they did not miss anything during their stay in Carmel. Inquire of your servants, and they will inform you. So please favor my servants in your eyes, for we have come on a festive day. Please give the servants and your son David whatever you have.' When David's young men arrived, they told Nabal all of this in David's name, and then they waited. "Who is David?" Nabal asked David's servants. "What is the name of Jesse's son? Many servants are rebelling against their masters these days. So, should I give my bread and water, as well as the meat I slaughtered for my shearers, to men from who knows where?" As a result, David's servants returned from their journey. They repeated every word to him when they arrived.

The Philistines gathered their forces for war against Israel at that time. "Be assured, you and your men must go out with us in the camp to battle at Jezreel," Achish said to David. "Very well," David said to Achish, "you will see what your servant is capable of." "Good," Achish said to David. "I'll make you my lifelong bodyguard." "So now, please, listen to you maiden, and let me put a little bread in front of you.

Then eat to keep yourself going." "I will not eat," he said. His servants, as well as the woman, persuaded him otherwise. As a result, he gave in to their pressure and sat on the bed. In the house, the woman kept a fat calf. She slaughtered it in such haste. She made unleavened bread by kneading flour and baking it. Saul and his servants ate it after she brought it to them. After that, they got up and left that evening.

It is for those in Bethel, Ramoth Negev, Jattir, Aroer, Siphmoth, Eshtemoa, Racal, and the cities of the Jerahmeelites and the cities of the Kenites, as well as those in Hormah, Borashan, Attach, and Hebron. Jonathan, Abinadab, and Malachi-shua, Saul's sons, were killed by the Philistines when they overtook him and his sons. Saul lost the battle decisively. The archers then discovered him and shot him in the back. "Draw your sword and thrust me through," Saul said to his armor-bearer, "or these uncircumcised will thrust me through and abuse me." His armor-bearer, on the other hand, refused because he was terrified. As a result, Saul drew his own sword and slashed himself.

David sent messengers to the people of Jabesh-Gilead and told them, "May the Lord bless you because you have performed this act of faithfulness toward your lord Saul and buried him." May the Lord continue to show you his faithfulness and unwavering love. And I, too, will repay your loyalty in this regard. So be steadfast and brave, for your lord Saul is dead, and the house of Judah has anointed me as their king." However, the leader of Saul's army, Abner, son of Ner, captured Ishbosheth, son of Saul, and transported him to Mahanaim. He crowned him king of Gilead, the Ashurites, Jezreel, Ephraim, Benjamin, and all of Israel. Saul's uncle, Ishbosheth, was forty years old when he became king of Israel and reigned for two years.

On the other hand, the house of Judah remained loyal to David. David ruled the house of Judah in Hebron for seven years and six months. But from Mahanaim to Gibeon, Abner, son of Ner, and Ishbosheth, son of Saul, marched. As a result, David's followers and Joab, son of Zeruiah, marched out to meet them at Gibeon's pool. The pool divided them into two bands, one on one side and the other on the other. "Let the young men compete in front of us," Abner told Joab. Joab replied, "Let them come forward." Then they came forward and were counted as they passed: twelve Benjaminites of Ishbosheth, son of Saul, and twelve David's supporters. But after each one grabbed his opponent's head and thrust his sword into his opponent's side, they all fell together. The name Helkath-hazzurim was given to a place in Gibeon called Helkath-hazzurim.

The Benjaminites rallied behind Abner and gathered at the top of a hill as a single force. Then Abner addressed Joab, saying, "Must the sword devour forever?" Do you not see how bitter it will be in the end? How long before you tell your troops to stop hunting down their relatives?" "As God lives, if] you hadn't spoken, the troops would have pursued their kinsmen until morning," Joab replied. 28 When Joab blew the trumpet, his troops came to a halt.

They didn't pursue Israel any further, and the fighting ended. Abner and his men marched through the Arabah all night, crossing the Jordan and marching through all of Bithron until they arrived at Mahanaim.

After Joab abandoned his pursuit of Abner, he gathered all his troops, and David's followers were missing nineteen men, including Asahel. However, David's followers defeated Benjamin, and three hundred sixty of Abner's men died. They carried Asahel away and buried him in his father's tomb in Bethlehem. Joab and his men marched through the night until day broke at Hebron.

After that, the house of Saul and the house of David fought for a long time. While David's strength grew, Saul's house grew weaker by the day. David's sons were born in Hebron. Amnon by Ahinoam of Jezreel; Dalujah by Abigail the Carmelite; Absalom the son of Maacah, daughter of King Talmai of Geshur; Adonijah the son of Haggith; Shephatiah by Abital; and Ithream by David's wife Eglahthese were all born in Hebron to David. Throughout the war between the houses of Saul and David, Abner consolidates his power in the house of Saul. Jonathan, Saul's son, now had a son with lame feet. When the news of Saul and Jonathan arrived from Jezreel, he was five years old, and his nurse picked him up and fled. He fell and became lame in her haste to flee. Mephibosheth was his name.

Saul is well, the Lord be praised, who told him: "'Now, Saul has been saved.', and Rechab and his brother Baanah, the sons of Rimmon the Beerothite, picked him up and they killed him. How much more so when a righteous man is murdered in his own home while he is sleeping! Do you honestly believe I'm not going to demand his blood and wipe you off the face of the planet?" David gave the young men orders to kill them, and they did so by chopping off their hands and feet and hanging them beside the pool in Hebron. He then took Mephibosheth's head and buried it in Hebron alongside Abner's grave.

Then, in the evening, David rose from his couch and went for a walk on the palace's roof. He saw a woman bathing from the roof, and she was beautiful. As a result, David dispatched messengers to inquire about the woman. "Isn't she Bathsheba, daughter of Eliam, wife of Uriah the Hittite, Joab's armorbearer?" someone asked.

Then David dispatched messengers to bring her to him, and she arrived purified, and he lay with her. She then went back to her house. But the woman became pregnant and sent David a message saying, "I am with child." "Send me Uriah the Hittite," David said to Joab, and Joab sent Uriah to David. When Uriah arrived, David inquired about Joab's health, the troops' performance, and the war's progress. "Go to your house and wash your feet," David told Uriah. When Uriah left the palace, the king dispatched a banquet for him.

Then, while Joab was laying siege to the city, he assigned Uriah to a location where he knew skilled warriors could be found. The citizens of the city came out to fight Joab. Some of David's army, as well as Uriah the Hittite, were killed. When Joab sent word to David, instructing the messenger, "When you have finished reporting to the king all about the battle if the king becomes angry and says to you, 'Why did you go so close to the city to fight?' 'Didn't you see that they were going to shoot from the wall?'

"I have sinned against the Lord," David confessed to Nathan. "The Lord has also forgiven your sin—you will not die," Nathan told David. However, because you have despised the Lord's word by this act, the child you have borne will undoubtedly perish." Nathan then went back to his house. God struck Uriah's child, whom David had borne. As a result, David prayed to God on the child's behalf. David fasted and entered the temple, where he lay in sackcloth on the ground.

The elders of his house came up to him and tried to persuade him to rise from the ground, but he refused and refused to eat with them. The child then died on the seventh day. During David's reign, there was a three-year famine. "It is because of the bloodguilt of Saul and his house because he put the Gibeonites to death," the Lord replied when David inquired.

The Philistines attacked Israel once more. David and his troops descended upon the Philistines and engaged them in battle. David grew tired of it. Ishbibenob, a descendant of the giants with a three-hundred-shekel spear, was enraged and plotted to kill David. But Abishai, son of Zeruiah, came to his aid and killed the Philistine. "You will never go to battle with us again so that you do not [put out the lamp of Israel," David's men swore.

After that, there was another battle with the Philistines, in which Sibbecai the Hushathite killed Saph, a giant's descendant. When the angel reached out to destroy Jerusalem, the Lord stopped the calamity and said to the angel who was destroying the people, "That is enough." Now put your hand down." The Lord's angel was standing by Araunah, the Jebusite's threshing floor. When David raised his eyes, he saw the Lord's angel standing between the earth and the heavens, his drawn sword in his hand stretching out toward Jerusalem. Covered in sackcloth, David and the elders collapsed to the ground. "Was it not I who ordered the census of the people?" David asked the Lord. Look, I've sinned and done a lot of bad things.

"As the Lord lives, who has delivered me from every adversity, just as swore to you by the Lord the God of Israel— 'Solomon your son will reign after me, he will sit on my throne in my stead'—today I will accomplish that!" the King declared. "Let my lord King David live forever," Bathsheba bowed, face to the ground, prostrating herself before the King.

"Call Zadok the priest, Nathan the prophet, and Benaiah son of Jehoiada," King David said. "Take your lord's servants with you, have Solomon my son ride on my mule, and lead him down to Gihon," the King said when they arrived in his presence. The priest Zadok and the prophet Nathan are to anoint him as King of Israel there. Then sound the trumpet and say "Long live King Solomon!" Then follow him back up to my throne, and he will sit on my throne. For he will rule in my place; he is the prince over Israel and Judah whom I have appointed." "Amen!" said Benaiah, the son of Jehoiada, in response to the King. May the Lord, my Lord the King's God, declare it. May the Lord be with Solomon as he has been with my Lord the King. May he make his throne even more powerful than my Lord King David's throne.

Thus, all of King Solomon's work on the Lord's temple was finished. Then Solomon acquired the sacred treasure from his father and stored i in the treasuries in the temple. Then the elders of Israel, all the leaders o the tribes, and tribal chiefs from the city of David assembled in Jerusalem to bring the Ark of the Covenant up to the city. At the time of the feast all of Israel gathered to King Solomon. The elders of Israel all arrived, and the ark was brought up. The priests and Levites had set up the tent and everything inside it.

King Solomon and the entire congregation of Israel who had gathered to him sacrificed so many sheep and oxen that they could not be counted or numbered before the ark. The priests carried the ark of the Lord's covenant into the temple's inner sanctuary, to the most holy place, under the cherubim's wings.

Because the cherubim spread their wings over the ark and its poles, the ark and its poles were completely covered. The poles were so long that they could be seen from the holy place in front of the inner sanctuary, even though they were not visible from the outside. They're still standing today. Except for the two stone tablets that Moses placed in the ark at Horeb when the Lord made a covenant with the Israelites when they fled Egypt, there was nothing else in the ark.

After consulting with his advisors, the King created two gold calves. "It is too much for you to travel to Jerusalem," he told them. Take a look at your gods, Israel, who brought you up out of Egypt." He established one in Bethel and the other in Dan. This became a sin because people traveled all the way to Dan to worship before the one who was there. Except for the Levites, he built shrines for the high places and appointed priests from among the people.

When the lepers reached the camp's edge, they gathered to eat and drink in one tent. They then took silver, gold, and clothing and went off to hide them. When they returned, they entered] another tent and took loot from it before going to hide it.

"What we're doing isn't right," they said to one another. We have some good news today, but we're keeping it to ourselves. We will be punished if we wait until the morning light. Let us go tell the rest of the King's household." So they came and told the city's gatekeepers, "We went into the Syrians' camp and saw that there was no one there, not a human voice, but the horses and donkeys were tied, and the tents remained just as they had been." And so it was with him. At the gate, the people trampled him, and he died, just as the man of God had predicted.

"Gird up your loins, take this vial of oil in your hand, and go to Ramoth-Gilead," Elisha, the prophet, told one of the prophetic group. Find Jehu, son of Jehoshaphat, son of Nimshi, when you arrive. Then take him to a private room and have him leave his associates." Jehu sent word throughout Israel, and all of Baal's worshipers came, so there was no one left who didn't come.

ISAIAH

In the days of Uzziah, Jotham, Ahaz, and Yehizqiyah, kings of Judah, Isaiah, son of Amoz, saw a vision concerning Judah and Jerusalem. Heavens, listen, and earth, hear, for the Lord has spoken. I have nurtured and raised children, but they have rebelled against me. The ox recognizes its owner, and the ass recognizes its master's manager; Israel does not, and my people do not comprehend. Oh, wretched nation, wretched people, seed of evildoers, wretched children. They have turned their backs on the Lord, despising Israel's Holy One. They've become estranged and regressed.

Why would you continue to rebel despite being beaten? The entire brain is sick, and the entire heart is weak. There are no healthy spots from the sole of the foot to the top of the head, only bruises, sores, and bleeding wounds that have not been pressed out, bound up or softened with oil. Your country is desolate, your cities are on fire, and your land is being devoured right in front of your eyes by foreigners. They have wreaked havoc on it as if foreigners had overthrown it. And Zion's daughter has been reduced to a hut in a vineyard, a shelter in a cucumber field, and a besieged city. We would have become like Sodom and Gomorrah if the Lord of hosts had not left us with a few survivors.

Sodom's rulers, and Gomorrah's people, pay attention to the Lord's word and our God's instruction! What level of self-sacrifice have you made for me? Declares the Lord. I've had my fill of fattened beasts and ram sacrifices. I am not a fan of the blood of bulls, lambs, or goats. Who has compelled you to trample my courts in order to see my face? Don't continue to bring meaningless gifts! Incense is an abomination to me. I can't stand iniquity with the solemnity of the new moon and Sabbath, the calling of meetings. Your new moons and feasts irritate me. They've become a burden I don't want to bear. I will turn away from you when you spread your hands in front of you. I will not listen to a thousand prayers. Your palms are contaminated with sin, and your hands are stained with blood.

Remove the evil of your actions from my sight by washing and making yourself clean. Stop being evil and start being good. Seek justice, assist those who have been injured, obtain justice for orphans, and defend widows. The Lord says, "Come now, and let us reason together." Even if your sins are scarlet, they will be as white as snow; even if they are crimson red, they will be as wool. You will eat the good of the land if you are willing and obey. However, if you refuse and rebel, you will be devoured by the sword because the Lord's mouth has spoken. Seven women will seize one man on that day and declare, "We will eat our own bread and wear our own clothes." Allow us to be addressed only by your name. "Remove our embarrassment."

On that day, the Lord's branch will be beautiful and glorious, and the land's fruit will be the pride and boast of Israel and Judah's escaped remnant. When my Lord has washed away the filth of Zion's daughters and cleansed Jerusalem's body by the Spirit of Judgment, whoever remains in Zion will be called holy, and those who come to dwell in Jerusalem will be sanctified. The Lord will place a canopy over the city and its multitude to preserve them from the sun's rays.

I saw my Lord sitting on his throne, high and exalted, in the year that King Uzziah died, and the skirts of his robe filled the temple. Seraphs with six wings stood above him. Two of them shielded their faces, two of them shielded their feet, and two of them flew. "Holy, holy is the Lord of hosts: the whole earth is full of his glory," they called out, shaking the foundations of the thresholds and filling the house with smoke. "Woe is me!" I exclaimed. I'm lost because I'm a man with unclean lips who lives among people who have unclean lips. Indeed, my eyes have seen the King, the Lord of hosts," one of the seraphs said, flying to me with a live coal in his hand, which he had taken with tongs from the altar. "Now that this has touched your lips," he said, "your iniquity is removed, and your sins are forgiven." And I heard my Lord say, "Whom will I send, and who will go for us?"

Then I said, "Here am I; send me." He replied, "Go, and say to this people: Hear, but do not comprehend; see, but do not comprehend." Make this people's hearts fat, their ears dull, and their eyes blind, so they can't see with their eyes, hear with their ears, understand with their hearts, or turn back and be healed."

"How long, Lord?" I asked. "Until the land becomes utterly desolate, and the Lord banishes the inhabitants, and desolate places multiply in the midst of the land, until cities lie waste, without inhabitant, and houses without occupant, and the land becomes utterly desolate, and the Lord banishes the inhabitants, and desolate places multiply in the midst of the land," he replied. Even if a tenth remains in it, it will be burned, as a terebinth or oak whose stump remains after it has been felled." The holy seed is its stump. The one carrying out unjust laws and issuing documents for the disadvantage of the needy; rob the poor of their rights so that orphanages will become their gain! What will you do on the day of your punishment, when disaster strikes from afar? 4 To avoid sinking under those in chains and falling under the slain, to whom will you turn for help, and where will you leave your wealth? Despite this, his anger is not turned away, and his hands are still stretched out.

Misery shall meet you! I'm the personification of their wrath. I will send him against a wicked and profane people, and I will empower him to deal harshly with them. Because the Lord has pity on Jacob, he will remain faithful to his covenant and make them strong. And many nations will grasp them and be given to the House of Judah as house-slaves and concubines in the Lord's land. Those who were oppressed by the majority will become their oppressors.

I will rise up against them, declares the Lord of hosts, and will cut off Babylon's name, remnant, offspring, and posterity.

The Lord of Hosts says that he will give it to the hedgehog to the hedgehog, too. Surely as I intended, so shall it be. When I go to my land, shall completely crush the Assyrian. He will then set you free and free you The Moabite oracle of Ar has been accomplished in a single night; the answer is: The Moab has been consumed and reduced to ashes. They are going to cry in the high places of Bayith and Dibon. Every hair is gone They walk around dressed in sackcloth, and everyone complains in the marketplaces.

According to the oracle, Damascus will no longer be a city but will become a heap of ruins. Otaru's cities are deserted; they will serve a resting places for flocks, with no one to frighten them. In Ephraim fortresses will be destroyed, and the kingdom in Damascus will be destroyed. According to the Lord of hosts, the remnant of Syria will be like the glory of the children of Israel; on that day, Jacob's glory will be diminished, and his body's health will be diminished. The oracle concerning Egypt: Behold, the Lord is approaching Egypt on a swift cloud. The Egyptian idols will tremble in his presence, and the Egyptians hearts will melt within them. And I'll turn Egyptians against Egyptians pitting brother against brother, neighbor against neighbor, city against city and kingdom against kingdom. The Egyptians' spirit will break down within them, and I will thwart their plans. They will seek advice from idols, dead spirits, mediums, and spiritists. The Egyptians will be delivered into the hands of a cruel master, and a fierce king will rule over them declares the Lord God of hosts. The oracle regarding the seaside pasture It comes from the desert, from a faraway land, as whirlwinds sweep through the Negev. I've been shown a terrifying vision in which the traitor betrays, and the destroyer destroys. Ascend, Elam, and lay siege to Media I'm putting an end to all the groaning she's been causing. As a result, my loins are in excruciating pain, and pangs have seized me like the pangs of a woman giving birth.

You are my God, Lord! I will exalt and praise your name because you have accomplished great things, plans that have been formed in faithfulness and truth over time.

Because you have reduced the city to ruins, the fortified city to ruins, and the foreigners' palace to ruin, it will never be rebuilt. As a result, powerful peoples will praise you, and cities of ruthless nations will fear you. You have been a haven for the poor, a refuge for the distressed, a shelter from the storm and the heat. Because the ruthless' breath is like a storm against a wall or heat in a dry place. The ruckus of foreigners will be subdued by the shade of clouds, just as the heat of the sun will be subdued by the shade of the clouds; the ruthless' song will be silenced.

Woe to those who seek help in Egypt and rely on horses, and trust in chariots because they are numerous, and in horsemen, because they are powerful—but do not look to the Holy One of Israel or seek the Lord! Yet he is wise, and he will bring disaster, and he will not regret his words, but he will arise against the house of the evildoers and against the assistance of those who work iniquity. Nations come closer to hear, and people, pay attention. Allow the earth and everything on it to hear, as well as the world and everything it produces, because the Lord is enraged with all the nations and their armies. He's doomed them, and he's determined to slaughter them. Their slain and corpses will be cast down, and the stench of their death will rise. Stabilize the stumbling knees and strengthen the shaky hands. "Be strong, do not fear; see, your God will bring vengeance, he will bring divine recompense to save you," say to those who are discouraged. The blind will be able to see again, and the deaf will be able to hear again. 6 The lame will then leap like a deer, and the mute tongue will sing.

For the Lord says, "Maintain justice and do what is right, for my salvation will come soon, and my deliverance will come soon." Blessed are those who do this, and those who keep it fast, who keep the Sabbath holy without profaning it, and who keep their hands from doing evil.

And I will not remain silent, and I will not stay silent for Jerusalem's sake until her vindication shines like the dawn and her salvation burns brightly. People will call you by a new name that the Lord's mouth will bestow.

The nations will see your vindication, and all the kings will see your glory. You will be a royal diadem in the Lord's hand and a crown of splendor in the Lord's hand. And you will no longer be referred to as Deserted, and your land will no longer be referred to as desolate; instead, people will refer to you as My delight is in her, and your land is wed; for the Lord delights in you, and your land is wed. Heaven is my throne, and the earth is my footstool, declares the Lord. Where is the house you said you'd build for me, and where will I be buried? All of these things were created by my hand, and as a result, all of these things exist, says the Lord. But it is he who is humble and contrite in spirit, and who trembles at my word, whom I will look upon.

JEREMIAH

The LORD commanded Jeremiah to stand at the LORD's gate and say to all the people who were entering through these gates, "Hear the word of the LORD."

I will banish you just as I have done to your brethren, the descendants of Ephraim. That means do not pray for them, do not make pleas, and do not intercede on their behalf because I refuse to hear you. Do you not see what they are doing in Judah and in Jerusalem? Enrage me, the children gather wood, light a fire, and then pour libations to other gods. Am I the one being provoked? Is it their own fault, but them?

You will tell them all of these things, but they will not listen. You must declare to them, "This is the nation that spurned the LORD God and so lost their self-discipline that they no longer accept the instruction." Cut your hair and mourn, for the Lord has rejected this generation.

The bones of the kings of Judah, the bones of its princes, the bones of the priests, the bones of the prophets, and the bones of the inhabitants of Jerusalem will be brought out of their graves at that time, says the LORD. Then they will spread them before the sun and all the stars, whom they have loved and served, and whom they have followed, consulted and worshipped. They will not be gathered or buried but will instead appear as dung on the ground's surface. And death, says the LORD of hosts, will be preferred to life by all the remnant [of this evil family] who remain in all the places where I have scattered them.

O house of Israel, pay attention to the word that the LORD speaks to you. The LORD says, "Do not learn the ways of the nations, and do not be alarmed by the signs of the heavens," because the nations are alarmed by them. Because the people's customs are false, they are a tree felled in the forest, the work of a craftsman's hands with an ax. They adorn it with silver and gold and secure it with hammer and nails to prevent it from moving.

113

The Lord spoke to Jeremiah, saying, "Hear the words of this covenant, and speak to the people of Judah and the people of Jerusalem." You shall say to them, "Cursed be anyone who does not hear the words of this covenant, which I commanded your forefathers when I brought them out of the land of Egypt, from the iron-smelting furnace, saying: Listen to my voice and do everything that I command you." So you will be my people, and I will be your God so that I can fulfill the oath I made to your forefathers to give them a land flowing with milk and honey, as it is today. Then I responded with, "Amen, LORD!" Then the LORD said to me, 'proclaim all these words in Judah's towns and in Jerusalem's streets: Hear the words of this covenant and carry them out.'

When King Zedekiah sent Pashhur, son of Malkijah, and the priest Zephaniah son of Maaseiah, to Jeremiah, the LORD spoke to him, saying:

Then, declares the LORD, I will deliver King Zedekiah of Judah, his servants, and the people of this city—those who survive the pestilence and the sword—to King Nebuchadrezzar of Babylon, their enemies, and those who seek their lives. He will slay them with the sword's edge; he will not spare them, nor will he have mercy or compassion for them. However, you did not listen to me, so you provoked me to anger with your handiwork to your own detriment, says the LORD.

Therefore, thus says the LORD of the kingdoms of the house of hosts, "Because you have not listened to My words, I will send for all the peoples of the north, My servant Nebuchadnezzar of Babylon, and I will bring them against this land and these nations and nations around against this land." I will utterly destroy them and make them an object of horror, scorn, and an everlasting disgrace.

Then in those days, and then on that occasion, I will initiate a good tree for David, and he will govern the land with justice and righteousness. In those days, Judah will be saved, and Jerusalem will live in safety. Here is the name by which I promise that it will be known: "The LORD our righteousness. For thus says the LORD: The King of Israel, The True Priest will never depart from his throne or anoints the priests who offer burnt offerings and sacrifices." But, my servant Jacob, do not be afraid, and do not be discouraged, O Israel! For see, I am going to save you from far away and your offspring from the land of their captivity. Jacob will be safe and secure when he returns, and no one will be able to scare him. Have no fear, my servant Jacob, for I am with you, declares the LORD. but you will not be destroyed!" Even so, I shall not leave you unpunished.

Before Pharaoh attacked Gaza, the LORD spoke to the prophet Jeremiah concerning the Philistines. See, waters are rising from the north, and they will become an overflowing torrent, overflowing the land and everything in it, the city and those who live in it, says the LORD. The people will scream, and the land's inhabitants will weep.

[The children of Israel, as well as the children of Judah,] will come in those days and at that time, says the LORD. They will weep as they travel in search of the LORD, their God. "Come, let us join ourselves to the LORD in an everlasting covenant that will not be forgotten," they will say as they ask the way to Zion with their faces turned toward it.

My people have become lost sheep, and their shepherds have led them astray. They have returned from the mountains. They've gone from mountain to mountain, completely forgetting about their own resting place.

EZEKIEL

Human hands protruded from beneath their wings. The four of them had faces and wings on each of their four sides. Their wings brushed up against each other. Each of them walked straight ahead, not turning.

There were three different faces: on the right, on the left, and on the other side. These were their facial expressions. Two wings touched each other and the other covered their bodies as they spread their wings upward. They all took a step forward. They didn't turn around and followed the Spirit wherever it went. The likeness of the living beings, and their appearance, was like burning coals of fire, like the light of torches. The fire was passed back and forth between the living beings. It was a bright fire that flashed with lightning. The living beings flew back and forth like bolts of lightning.

I noticed one wheel on the ground beside each of the four living beings when I looked at them. The appearance and construction of the wheels were as follows: They glistened like chrysolite, were identical in form and construction, and appeared to be a wheel within a wheel. They could move in any of the four directions they wanted without turning.

Then I noticed four wheels beside the cherubim, one beside each of the cherubim. The wheels had a chrysolite gleam to them. In terms of appearance, they all appeared to be the same, like a wheel within a wheel. They could move in any of the four directions they wanted without turning. Wherever the lead wheel pointed, the others followed without turning. Their entire body, backs, hands, wings, and the four wheels of the four of them were covered in eyes. The wheels were referred to as "the whirling wheels"]. Each one had four faces: the first was a cherub's face, the second was a man's face, the third was a lion's face, and the fourth was an eagle's face.

The cherubim rose to their feet. These were the living creatures I encountered along the Chebar River. The wheels moved alongside the cherubim when they moved, and they did not leave their side when the cherubim spread their wings to rise from the ground.

When these remained motionless, those remained motionless as well; when these rose, those rose with them because the Spirit of the living beings was in them. Now you, Mortal, prophesy to the mountains of Israel, saying, "Hear the word of the LORD, mountains of Israel." Because the enemy has said to you, "Aha!" and "The ancient heights have become our possession," prophesy and say, "This is what the Lord GOD says: Because they have made you desolate and crushed you on every side so that you have become a possession to the rest of the nations and the subject of gossip and slander among the people; therefore, mountains of Issachar have become our possession."

Therefore, tell the house of Israel: "This is what the LORD says: I am not acting for your sake, but for holy for all the nations, that you have made polluted this. The nations will see my holiness and know that I am the LORD," Psalms 69:6:10 I shall take you and lift you up from all the nations and settle you in your own land. Make you holy. Everything foul and profane will be swept away. I will make you whole again. The LORD's hand was on me, and the LORD led me out, and I was in the valley, which was full of bones. He tricked me into following him. Many of them were on the floor and very dusty "Can these bones survive?" "God knows,"

"Prophesy over these bones, and say to them, Dry bones, hear the word of the LORD," he said. Listen to what the Lord GOD has to say to these bones; I'll force air into your lungs, and you'll live. I will attach tendons to you, form flesh, cover you with skin, and breathe into you, and you will live. Then you'll realize I'm the LORD." As a result, I prophesied as instructed. There was a rattling and a noise, just as I predicted. The bones came together, one after the other. Sinews and flesh formed on them as I watched, and skin covered them, but they didn't have any breath. "Prophesy to the wind; prophesy to the wind, Mortal, and say to the wind, this is what the Lord GOD says: Come from the four winds, breathe, and breathe on these slain, that they may come to lie," he said. As he instructed, I prophesied, and breath entered them, and they came to life and stood up on their feet—a massive army.

Hosea

She became pregnant again and gave birth to a daughter. "Name her Lo-ruhamah," the LORD said to him, "for I will no longer have mercy on the house of Israel that I should pardon them in any way." But I will have mercy on the house of Judah, and I will save them through the LORD their God, not through the bow, sword, battle, horses, or horsemen."

She conceived and gave birth to a son after she had weaned Lo-ruhamah. "Name him Lo-Ammi," the LORD said, "for you are not my people, and I am not your God."

Yet the number of the children of Israel will be as the sand of the sea, which cannot be measured] or counted; and then he will say to them, "You are the sons of the living God," in the place where it was said to them, "You are not my people." And the children of Judah and the children of Israel will be gathered together, and they will choose one leader and depart from the land; for the day of Jezreel will be great.

"Go again, love a woman who has a lover and is an adulteress, just as the LORD loves the children of Israel, even though they turn to other gods and love raisin cakes," the LORD said to me. So I bought her for fifteen pieces of silver, a homer of barley, and a lethech of barley and told her, "You shall remain with me for many days; you shall not play the harlot, and you shall not have a man, so will I be toward you." Israel's children will be without a king or prince for many days and without a sacrifice or pillar, an ephod, or a teraphim. After that, the children of Israel will return to seek the LORD their God and David, their king, and in the latter days, they will come with fear to the LORD and to His goodness.

Do not rejoice like the peoples, O Israel, for you have played the harlot, turning away from your God. On every grain floor, you've lusted after a prostitute's wages. They will go hungry on the threshing floor and in the winepress, and the new wine will fail them. They will not stay in the LORD's land; instead, Ephraim will return to Egypt and eat unclean food in Assyria.

They shall not offer drink offerings to the LORD, nor shall their sacrifices be acceptable to him. Their bread will be like mourners' bread; all who eat it will be defiled; for their bread will be for their own appetites; it will not enter the LORD's house.

Take your words with you and return to the LORD. "Take away all iniquity, accept what is good, and we will offer the fruit of our lips," say to him. Assyria will not save us; we will not ride on horses; we will no longer say to our creations, "You are our gods." For the orphan finds mercy in you."

Because my anger has turned away from them, I will heal their apostasy and freely love them. To Israel, I will be like dew; he will blossom like a lily, and his roots will sprout like Lebanon. What do I have to do with idols, Ephraim? I, too, have responded and observed him. I'm like a lush cypress, and it's from me that you get your fruit. Who is wise enough to comprehend these things? Prudent, so that he may be aware of them? The LORD's ways are correct, and the righteous will walk in them; however, transgressors will stumble in them.

JOEL

Sound an alarm on my holy mountain by blowing the trumpet in Zion. Let all the people of the land tremble, for the day of the LORD is approaching; a day of darkness and gloom, a day of clouds and thick darkness, as the dawn spreads across the mountains; a great and powerful people; there has never been anything like it, and there will never be again, for many generations. A fire consumes them in front of them while a flame burns behind them. The land is like the Garden of Eden in front of them and a desolate wilderness behind them. They will not be able to escape. Their appearance is similar to that of horses, and they run like war horses. They leap from the tops of the mountains like chariots, like the sound of a flame devouring the stubble, as a mighty army arrayed for battle. The people in front of them are in agony, and everyone's face has turned pale. They run like powerful men; they scale the wall like soldiers; and they march in single file, with no breaks in the ranks. And they don't push each other; everyone marches in his own direction, and they burst through the weapons without breaking ranks.

Fear not, O land; rejoice and be glad because the LORD has done great things for you. Fear not, you field animals; the wilderness pastures have turned green, the tree has produced fruit, and the fig tree and vine have yielded abundantly. So rejoice in the LORD your God, O children of Zion, for he has given you the former rain for your vindication, and he has showered you with rain, the former rain, and the latter rain as before. And you shall eat and be satisfied, and you shall praise the LORD your God, who has dealt wondrously with you; my people shall never be ashamed. And you shall know that I am in Israel, that I am the LORD your God, and that there is no one else; my people shall never be ashamed. I will then pour out my Spirit on all flesh; your sons and daughters will prophesy, your old men will dream dreams, and your young men will see visions. In those days, I will also pour out my Spirit upon the male and female servants. And I will perform miracles in the heavens and on the earth, such as blood, fire, and smoke pillars.

The mountains will drip sweet wine, the hills will flow with milk, and all the brooks of Judah will flow with water on that day, and a fountain will spring forth from the LORD's house, watering the entire valley of Shittim. Because of the violence perpetrated against the children of Judah, and because they have shed innocent blood in their land, Egypt will be a desolation, and Edom will be a wilderness, a desolate wilderness. On the other hand, Judah will be inhabited for all time, and Jerusalem will be inhabited from generation to generation. Because the LORD dwells in Zion, I will avenge their blood that I have not avenged.

AMOS

Thus says the LORD, for the fourth time: I will not revoke Damascus' punishment because it has threshed the women of Gilead with iron tools; thus, the palaces of Bend will be set ablaze, and I will shatter the bars of Damascus, as well as the one who rules over it, the LORD tells.

Because they carried into exile the entire people to deliver them up to Edom, [I will not revoke their punishment] for three transgressions of Gaza, and for four, I will not revoke their punishment. So I'm going to set fire to Gaza's wall, and it'll burn down its palaces. And I will cut off the inhabitant of Ashdod and the scepter-bearer of Ashkelon, and I will turn my hand against Ekron, and the Philistines will perish, says the Lord GOD.

Should two people walk together unless they have an appointment? Will a lion roar in the woods if he has no prey? If a young lion hasn't caught anything, will he scream from his den? Will a bird fall into a snare set on the ground if there is no bait? Is it possible for a trap to spring up from the ground when it has taken nothing? Will a city's inhabitants be afraid if a trumpet is blown? Will a city be destroyed unless the LORD has decreed it? Indeed, unless the Lord GOD reveals his secret to his prophets, he will do nothing. Who will not be afraid now that the lion has roared? Who can but prophesy now that the Lord GOD has spoken?

"Assemble yourselves upon the mountains of Samaria, and see what great tumults [are in it, and what oppressions are in its midst," proclaim to the palaces of Ashdod and the palaces of Egypt. Those who store up violence and robbery in their palaces do not know how to do right, declares the Lord GOD. As a result, says the LORD, an adversary will surround the land, robbing you of your strength and plundering your palaces. Strike the capitals so that the thresholds shake and shatter them on the heads of all of them, and I will slay the last of them with the sword. I saw the Lord standing beside the altar. None of them will be able to flee, and none of them will be able to escape.

Even if they dig into Sheol, my hand will take them there; even if they climb to heaven, I will bring them down from there. I will search for them on the top of Carmel and take them from there; if they are hidden from my sight at the bottom of the sea, I will command the serpent to bite them there. Even if their enemies take them captive, I will command the sword from there, slay them, and fix my gaze on them for evil rather than good.

OBADIAH

For the day of the LORD is drawing near for all the nations; what you have done will be done to you; your dealings will come back to haunt you. For just as you drank on my holy mountain, so [shall] all nations drink incessantly; indeed, they shall drink and swallow down and be as if they had never been. Those who escape will be found on Mount Zion, which will be holy, and the house of Jacob will possess those who possess them. And the house of Jacob will be a fire, and the house of Joseph will be a flame, and the house of Esau will be stubble, and they will burn among them and devour them, and the house of Esau will have no survivor; for the LORD has spoken. And the Negev will possess Esau's mount, and the Philistines will possess the lowlands, and they will possess Ephraim's land and Samaria's land, and Benjamin will possess Gilead. And the exiles of the children of Israel who are among the Canaanites as far as Zarephath, and the exiles of Jerusalem who are in Sepharad, shall possess the cities of the Negev; and] deliverers shall ascend Mount Zion to judge Esau's mountain, and the kingdom shall be the LORD's.

JONAH

"Arise, go to Nineveh, that great city, and cry against it, for their wickedness has come up before me," the LORD said to Jonah, the son of Amittai. But Jonah rose up to flee Tarshish from the LORD's presence, and he went down to Joppa, where he found a ship [going to Tarshish, paid its fare, and boarded it to flee Tarshish from the LORD's presence. However, the LORD blew a strong wind across the sea, causing a violent storm, and the ship was about to capsize. The sailors were terrified, and each one cried out to his god, and they threw the ship's cargo into the sea to lighten it for them. On the other hand, Jonah had gone down into the ship's hold, lain down, and was fast asleep. As a result, the shipmaster approached him and asked, "What are you doing sleeping?" Get up and make a prayer to your god. Perhaps the god will notice us, and we will not perish."

From the belly of the fish, Jonah prayed to the LORD his God. And he said, "I cried out to the LORD in my distress, and he answered me; [I cried out from Sheol's belly, and you heard my voice. Because you cast me deep into the heart of the seas, where the flood was all around me, and all your waves and billows passed over me. 'I have been cast out of your sight; how will I ever look at your holy temple again?' I said. The waters engulfed me; the deep encircled me; the weeds wrapped themselves around my head. I descended to the depths of the mountains, the earth's bars closing in on me forever; yet, O LORD my God, you have brought the life of my soul up from the pit. When my life began to fade within me, I remembered the LORD, and my prayer reached you, your holy temple. Those who worship false idols abandon their faith. But I will offer thanksgiving sacrifices to you and pay what I have promised. The LORD is the source of salvation." And after the LORD spoke to the fish, it vomited Jonah onto dry land.

And the word of the LORD came to Jonah again, saying, "Arise, go to Nineveh, that great city, and call out to it the message that I am about to tell you." So Jonah arose and went to Nineveh, according to the LORD's word. Nineveh, a three-day journey away, was now an exceedingly great city.

And Jonah began to walk into the city for one day, crying out, "Yet forty days, and Nineveh shall be overthrown." And the people of Nineveh believed God and called a fast, and everyone, great and small, dressed in sackcloth.

But it infuriated Jonah, and he became enraged. "I pray, O LORD, was this not what I said while I was still in [my own] country?" he prayed to the LORD. As a result, I initially fled to Tarshish, knowing that you are a gracious and merciful God, slow to anger and abundant in loving-kindness, and one who relents in the face of evil. "Are you right to be angry over the plant?" God asked Jonah. " And he said, "It is right that I am angry, even to death." And the LORD said, "You have been concerned about the plant, for which you have not labored or caused to grow; which came up in a night, and perished in a night." Shouldn't I be concerned about Nineveh, that great] city, where there are over a hundred and twenty thousand people who don't know their right hand from their left hand, as well as a large number of animals? "

MICAH

At that time, Micah was receiving the Word of the LORD during the reigns of Jotham, Ahaz, and the kings of Judah: Obey, you peoples, all of the peoples, and let the LORD hear you from his holy abode. The Lord is coming down from his heavenly seat and will appear on earth. And people will melt under pressure, like wax, and slope down like water. All of this is Jacob's fault. Why did Jacob offend? Is this Israel? Judah's holy mountain are. It sure is! As a result, I'll make Samaria into fields and vineyards.

Whoa, who they practice it in the morning because it is within their power. They covet fields and seize them, as well as houses and take them away, oppressing a man and his house, as well as a man and his inheritance. As a result, says the LORD, "Behold, I am devising evil against this family, from which you will not be able to remove their necks, nor shall you walk haughtily; for it is an evil time."

And I asked them, "Ladies and gentlemen, men of Israel, is it not to be just?" Do you dislike the good and hate the evil? You who have torn their flesh from their bones and have consumed their flesh; devoured their meat in the cauldron of your people.

Then they will begin to cry out to the LORD, but he will ignore them because of their wickedness. Who has shown you forgiveness and does not spare the wicked? Because he delights in being kind, he does not hold grudges. He will have mercy on us and rid us of all our sins. You will give Jacob respect and love as you've sworn to our forefathers for all time.

NAHUM

Isaiah Nahum's dream/vision in the book. Jealous and vengeful The LORD is always forgiving, and he stands over the storm and sways the dust of the earth. He scolds the sea, and all the rivers: Carmel, Bashan, and Lebanon will perish. Because of him, the mountains tremble, and the entire Earth shakes. Who can stop his anger? And who can face his wrath? He seethes with rage and pounds the rock into pieces. The LORD is a shelter from trouble.

Woe to the bloodthirsty metropolis! The prey never leaves the quarry, which is full of lies and plunder. The whirring of the whips, the stamping of the hooves, the sound of the horse's feet, the fighting, men charging, the rising gleam of weapons, and many falling corpses, and never stopping: she is an Ambassador of Scotia and responsible for family lineaments. I am against you, declares the LORD of hosts, and I will uncover your skirts over your face, and I will reveal your nakedness to the nations, and your shame to the kingdoms.

Habakkuk

Take a look at the countries, observe them, and be amazed! I'm amazed! Because I'm working on a project in your days that you won't believe despite what you've been told. For behold, I am raising up the Chaldeans, that wrathful and rash people who march across the globe to take possession of lands that are not theirs. They are terrible and dreadful; their dignity and judgment come from within. I'll stand on my watch and climb the tower, keeping an eye on him to see what he'll say to me and how I'll respond to his reproof. And the LORD replied to me, saying, "Write the vision, and make it plain on tablets, so that whoever reads it may run." Because the vision is still for the appointed time, it is speeding toward completion and will not fail. Wait for it, even if it takes a while because it will come; it will not be delayed. The proud one's soul is not right within him; however, the righteous will live by faith. Furthermore, wine betrays an arrogant man, causing him to leave the house. He expands his desire like Sheol and is like death; he cannot be satisfied, so he gathers all nations and peoples to himself.

Habakkuk's prophetic prayer set to Shigionoth. I'm afraid, O LORD because I've heard the news about you. O LORD, renew your work in the midst of the years; make it known in the midst of the years; remember mercy in wrath. Teman is the home of God, and Mount Paran is the home of the Holy One. Greetings! The heavens were engulfed in his glory, and the earth was replete with his praise. And his brilliance was as bright as the sun, with rays emanating from his hand, and it was there that his power was hidden. Pestilence washed over him, and fiery bolts rained down from the sky at his feet. He stood, saw, and shaped the earth; the nations shook at his feet; mountains prostrated themselves before him; he came and went, and the ages broke; he made what has already been created anew, and the eternal created things have their trembling." Cushan's tents were in distress, and the curtains of Midian's land shook.

ZEPHANIAH

In the days of Josiah, the son of Amon, king of Judah, the word of the LORD came to Zephaniah, the son of Cushi, the son of Gedaliah, the son of Amarah, the son of Hezekiah.

I will completely consume everything on the face of the earth, declares the LORD. I will consume man and animal; I will destroy the birds of the heavens, the fish of the sea, and the stumbling blocks of the wicked; and I will wipe man off the face of the earth, declares the LORD. And I will stretch out my hand upon Judah and all the inhabitants of Jerusalem, and I will cut off the remnant of Baal from this place, the name of the idolatrous priests with the priests; and those who worship, who swear to the LORD and swear by Milcom; and those who have not soured from following the LORD; and those who have not soured from following the LORD; and those who have not soured from following the LORD; and those who have not soured from following the LORD; and those.

Gather yourselves, yes, gather yourselves, O shameless nation; before the decree takes effect, the day passes as chaff, before the LORD's fierce anger comes upon you, before the LORD's day of wrath comes upon you. All you meek of the earth, who have kept the LORD's ordinances, seek the LORD; seek righteousness, seek humility; perhaps you will be hidden in the day of the LORD's wrath. For Gaza will be abandoned, and Ashkelon will be a desolation; they will drive Ashdod out at noon, and Ekron will be uprooted.

Woe to the Cherethites, the people who live along the coast! The LORD's word is against you, Canaan, the land of the Philistines; I will destroy you and leave no one to live there. And the seacoast will be pastures, shepherd caves, and flock folds.

Sing, O Zion's daughter; shout, O Israel's daughter; be glad and rejoice with all your heart, O Jerusalem's daughter. The LORD has removed your judgments; he has expelled your enemies; the King of Israel, even the LORD, is in your midst; [you shall no longer be afraid of evil. It will be said to Jerusalem on that day, "Fear not; O Zion, do not let your hands be slack."

The LORD your God, a mighty one who will save you, is in your midst; he will exult over you with singing; he will rejoice over you with joy; he will rest in his love; he will exult over you with joy. I'll gather those who were sad for the solemn assembly and who were of you, to whom the burden on her was an embarrassment. I will deal with all who afflict you at that time, save the lame and gather the scattered, and make them a praise and a name, whose shame has been all over the earth.

HAGGAI

The word of the LORD came to Zerubbabel, the son of Shealtiel, governor of Judah, and Joshua, the son of Jehozadak, the high priest, in the second year of Darius, the king, in the sixth month, on the first day of the month, saying, Thus says the LORD of hosts, saying, "This people says, 'The time has not come to rebuild the house of the LORD.'" The prophet Haggai then spoke for the LORD, saying, "Is it time for you to dwell in your paneled houses while this house lies waste?" As a result, the LORD of hosts says, "Consider your ways." You have sown much and brought in little; you eat, but not enough; you drink, but not enough; you clothe yourselves, but no one is warm, and he who earns wages, earns wages to put it into a hole-filled bag."

So declares the LORD of Hosts. "Think about what you're doing. "Go up to the mountain, bring wood, and construct the house; and I will rejoice over it, and I will be glorified," says the LORD. "You searched for a long time and found nothing, and when you brought it home, I blew it away. Why? Declares the LORD of hosts because my house is in ruins, and everyone is fleeing to his own home. As a result, the heavens withhold the dew, and the earth withholds its fruit for your sake.

The word of the LORD came to Haggai the prophet in the seventh month, on the twenty-first day of the month, saying, "Speak now to Zerubbabel the son of Shealtiel, governor of Judah, and Joshua, the son of Jehozadak, high priest, and to the remnant of the people, saying, 'Who is left among you who saw this house in its former glory?' And how do you think it's going now? Is it nothing in your eyes? But now, O Zerubbabel, be strong; and now, O Joshua, son of Jehozadak, the high priest; and now, all you people of the land, be strong, and work: for I am with you,' says the LORD of hosts, according to the word that I covenanted with you when you came out of Egypt, and my Spirit is abiding among you; do not fear.' " Because, as the LORD of hosts declares, "I will shake the heavens, the earth, the sea, and the dry land once more in a short while, and I will shake all nations; and the treasure of all nations shall come, and I will fill this house with glory," declares the LORD of hosts. "I own the silver and the gold," says the narrator.

The LORD of Hosts declares, "It is mine." "I will give peace in thi place," says the LORD of hosts, "and the latter glory of this house will be greater than the former glory."

ZECHARIAH

LORD spoke to Zecharaiachariah, the son of Bereshit, the prophet, saying, "The LORD was furious with your fathers." Therefore return to me, says the LORD of the hosts. In contrast, please don't be like your forefathers to whom the former prophets cried out, "thus says the LORD of hosts. Stop being evil and turn to goodness," Where are your fathers? Are prophets allowed to live forever? But were my statutes and the statutes of my observers not found among you? As he had done in the past, so would he do in the future.

"O my lord, what are these?" I asked. "I will show you what these are," the angel who spoke with me said. "These are those whom the LORD has sent to patrol the earth," the man who stood among the myrtle trees replied. "We have patrolled the earth, and behold, all the earth is at rest," they responded to the angel of the LORD who stood among the myrtle trees.

The LORD of Hosts shows envy toward Zion and rivalry with her. "I'll return to Zion," says the LORD, "and Jerusalem shall be called the Mountain of Truth." According to the LORD of hosts, elderly men and women will go about the city holding sticks in hand.

Damascus will be the final place of Hadashah's authority. The eyes of all the tribes of Canaan are toward the LORD, just as Tyre and Sidon were. Building a stronghold, Tyre collects dust and gold; while accumulating silver, she will be given to the Lord, and then she will be destroyed.

The LORD will also save Judah's tents first so that the glory of David's house and the glory of Jerusalem's inhabitants are not exalted above Judah. The LORD will defend the people of Jerusalem on that day, and he [who is feeble among them at the time] will be like David, and the house of David will be like God, as the angel of the LORD before them. Then I will seek to destroy all the nations that come against Jerusalem on that day.

And I will pour out the Spirit of grace and supplication upon the house of David, and upon the inhabitants of Jerusalem; and they shall look to me whom they have pierced, and they shall mourn for Him as one mourns for his only son, and they shall be bitter for him as one is bitter for his firstborn.

MALACHI

Therefore, now I shall send my Messenger, and he shall arrange the procedure for me: He shall arrive with great speed, the Messenger of the LORD; He says, "Look, LORD is here in his temple" But who can stand up to them when they arrive? Who will be left standing when he appears? Because he is like a refiner's fire and fuller's soap, he will sit as a refiner and purifier of silver, and he will purify and refine the sons of Levi as gold and silver, and they will offer to the LORD offerings in righteousness. Then the offering of Judah and Jerusalem will be pleasing to the LORD, as it was in the past and in previous years. And I will come near you for judgment; and I will be a swift witness against sorcerers, adulterers, and false swearers, and against those who oppress the hireling in his wages, the widow, and the orphan, and those who turn away the sojourner from his right, says the LORD God.

Behold, the day is coming; it is flaming as a furnace of fire, and all the evildoers shall be stubble, and their roots shall be destroyed. But the sun of righteousness will rise with healing in its wings for those who fear my name, and you will go forth and skip around like a stall calf. And you shall advise the wicked, for they shall be ashes under your feet in the day of the LORD of hosts, says the LORD of hosts. Remember my servant Moses' Law, which I gave him in Horeb for all Israel, including statutes and judgments. Before the great and terrible day of the LORD arrives, I will send you Elijah, the prophet. And he shall turn the hearts of fathers toward their children, and the hearts of children toward their fathers; otherwise, I will come and curse the earth.

Solomon wrote Solomon's Song. Make love to me with his lips!" Because of your affection, your scent is pleasing, and you have the most delicate of all names. People admire you because of this. Please, draw me after you. They've summoned me to the King's Chambers to praise your love. So true, my loved ones! "

Like Kedar's tents and Solomon's curtains, I am black and handsome. Do not gaze upon me because I've been burnt by the sun. Even though I neglected my own family, they chose me to take care of the vineyards. Invite me where you keep your sheep and sit with your sweetheart at noon. Why should I look like one of your flock who wears a veil?

Pay attention! My sweetheart! Here he comes, running over the hills and over the mountains. My lover has the appearance of a gazelle or a young stag. Look—standing he's behind our curtain, peering in through the lattice at the windows."

"Come here, fair one,' my lover says to me. Another example: For instance, the rain has stopped. Things are pleasant, the spring is here, and doves are cooing in our country. Consider how the fig tree and its blossom operate. Every night, I looked under my bed for my sweetheart. "I told myself, 'I'll get up right now and walk the city looking for my love" I found him, but couldn't find him.

"When the city watchmen came across me on their rounds, I asked, 'Have you seen the one my heart loves?' I had barely passed them by when I came across the one my heart desires!'

I didn't let go of him until I got him into my mother's house, into the room of the woman who gave birth to me. By the gazelles and the wild does, I charge you, daughters of Jerusalem: do not stir up or awaken love until it is ready!"

"How lovely your sandaled feet are, O prince's daughter!" Your thighs are shaped like jewels, the work of an artist's hands. Your navel is a rounded bowl filled with mixed wine at all times.

Your waist is surrounded by lilies and a mound of wheat. Your twin breasts resemble two fawns, like gazelle twins. Your neck resembles an ivory tower, and your eyes resemble the pools of Heshbon near Bath-gate. Your nose resembles the Lebanon Tower, which faces Damascus. Your flowing locks are like purple garments, and your head crowns you like (Mount) Carmel; a king is held captive by your tresses." And, my love, with all your charms, how fair and delightful you are! You have the stature of a palm tree, and your breasts resemble its fruit clusters. "I'll climb the palm tree and grab its date clusters," I said. Oh, may your breasts resemble grape clusters, and the scent of your breath resembles apples; may your kisses resemble the best wine that flows smoothly through lips and teeth."

Made in the USA
Las Vegas, NV
06 July 2023

74292098R10079